<u>G</u>o <u>U</u>ntil <u>T</u>ime <u>S</u>tops <u>Y</u>ou!

GUTSY

A Motivational Handbook

*Recovering the Power
with- 'IN.'*

by Matthew A. Forck

GUTSY (<u>Go</u> <u>Until</u> <u>Time</u> <u>Stops</u> <u>You!</u>)

GUTSY –_G_o _U_ntil _T_ime _S_tops _Y_ou!
Recovering the Power with-'IN.'

Copyright © 2006 Matthew A. Forck
All rights reserved.
No part of this book may be reproduced, stored in a retrieval
system or transmitted by any means, electronic, mechanical,
photocopying, recording or otherwise, without the written
permission from the author.

ISBN Number; 0-615-13441-6

Printed in the United States of America

Published by:

K-Crof Industries LLC, *dedicated to
building people through writing, speaking
and giving!*

Dedicated to two gutsy kids, Natalie & Nathan.
Thanks for the joy you bring to this world.

gut \ 'gət\ *n*: bowels or entrails as it relates to nourishment through the intestine or stomach or the emotional part of a person.

gut \ 'gət\ *adj* **gutsy**, -ier, -est: arising from within, from the innermost parts of the soul, having immediate and powerful impact, showing relevance, courage, brilliance, passion, determination, significance.

"Ah, to dream the dream
And stand in your youth by the starry stream.

Better yet to live life through
And say at the end, the dream came true."
Unknown.

At life's end we will say one of two things: "I wish I had" or "I'm glad I did." This book contains the seeds to "the dream came true" and "I'm glad I did." Plant the seeds, my friends; the best is yet to be.

GUTSY, an introduction...

An old proverb reads, "A journey of a thousand miles begins with just one step...take that first step today."

You have opened this book out of curiosity: you are demanding answers to one of two questions. It is possible that an older, well-dressed woman with some crazed look in her eye gave you a copy of this book and you are trying to find out why. You guess that the answer has to be somewhere between these covers. If that's the case, let me fill you in on a little secret. That was my mom. She has taken it upon herself to do everything she can to make my fourth book a New York Times best seller. She has personally purchased hundreds of books and is giving them out to her closest friends, neighbors, grocery store clerks, dry cleaners, bank tellers, et al. Thanks, Mom, for the support! For the rest of you, well you are curious too but for a different reason. You are looking for answers to different questions. Questions a little deeper than, "Who is this woman?" And, "Why is she handing me a book?"

I myself have been in search of answers. None more urgent than a few years back when I was asked to give the closing comments for a major safety conference. I was honored but overwhelmed...what message could I possibly send to this group of professionals after nearly six hours of top-notch speakers? Feeling overwhelmed, I thought it best to turn to procrastination. After all, the greatest labor saving device ever invented is tomorrow. Instead of searching the Internet for material for my speech, I turned to the last two boxes in the corner of my office closet. The fact that these boxes had been taped shut for the last two decades and positioned in the corner of this particular office closet since moving there didn't matter. It was finally time to unpack them. I really didn't want to write that speech.

And so I worked, shifting through the first box then cracking open the second. These boxes were a mix-match of college and high school, bringing back memories, thoughts and feelings that had been buried deep inside me for nearly as long as these boxes had been taped shut. You remember these times, don't you...back when life was simpler, easier and dreams seemed achievable? It was at the bottom of this second box, that I unearthed a long lost memento of the past. I pulled out two buckeye seeds, gripped them tight and smiled.

Buckeyes, you may know, are seeds from a buckeye tree just as acorns are the seeds from an oak tree. In Missouri buckeyes are somewhat unique and rare. These particular buckeyes were from the large tree that stood on the Missouri state capitol grounds. Almost a quarter of a century ago I stuffed them in my pockets as I waited for the city bus on a hot August afternoon. Back when I was in junior high school, a friend and I would catch the city bus to downtown Jefferson City. We would spend the day and all of our grass cutting money on baseball cards, cheap collector coins and hotdogs. But without fail at the end of each adventure, we would wait for the bus under the shade of this large buckeye tree. These buckeyes and my memories are all that remain of those carefree days.

As I sat in the darkened corner of my office closet, I stopped to picture that tree. Think of the biggest tree you can remember. I could vividly recall that old buckeye tree in my mind's eye. It was so big that there was no way I could reach my arms around the trunk. I remembered all of those leaves; so many that they could comfortably filter out even the hottest Missouri summer afternoon. Last I could see the thousands and thousands of buckeyes affixed to the branches each year. As I held these seeds in my hand reminiscing the past, it struck me...inside this tiny seed is a trunk so large that I couldn't wrap my arms around it, millions and millions of leaves and thousands and thousands of buckeyes. How did all of these things get in there, in this one tiny seed?

I realized at that moment that this tiny seed was hardwired for all of these things; you know, that large trunk, leaves and seeds. It is part of the package you get when you hold a buckeye seed. I realized at that same moment, there in the dark corner of my office closet, that in the very same way we hold inside of each of us, a potential to grow, bloom, expand and produce. That's part of our hardwiring, part of the package that is a person, each and every person. Do you really think that a person would be hardwired to a lesser extent than a simple buckeye seed? Of course not, inside each of us is pure greatness, success, selflessness, love and caring. I grinned widely as I had not only unearthed a long lost memory but closing remarks for a major conference.

Well, open this book and begin searching for answers to your questions. This book is like that long forgotten box in the closet corner. We all have them, and they haven't been opened for years. Yet we keep telling ourselves that some day we will look at these relics stored deep in the bottom of our heart, I mean box. You see the answers to the questions you have about life, happiness, dreams, goals and the drudgery that is day-to-day life can be found in that box...in this book. The purpose of this book is to lead you to success and significance through stories. To allow those seeds planted deep within you to be fertilized and you to grow, bloom, expand and produce or, as I like to say, get gutsy.

The book contains dozens and dozens of inspirational stories. Stories are a core of our being and the best means to being gutsy. Stories have been used for generations to teach. The generations before us huddled around campfires to listen to, share and learn from stories. In our lifetime alone reading such phrases as, "the three pigs, we aren't in Kansas anymore," and "Cinderella" can initial vivid memories. The importance of stores is highlighted in Thomas Moore's 2004 book entitled The Dark Nights of the Soul as he wrote, "The truth of things can only be expressed aesthetically, in story, picture, film, dance, music. Only when ideas are poetic do they reach the depths and express the reality."

These are stories for the next phase of our life...that gear that we need so that we can perspire and inspire before we expire. Gutsy is in the depths of our being, and taking that first step begins inside; reestablishing our dreams and just who we are. It then in-graves crucial values in our hearts and our lives. We begin to insist, determining how badly we want to be 'who we are.' To insist leads to inspire, where we find courage to work through setbacks. It is living in-choice, realizing that we create our lives instead of reacting to life. Gutsy is being in-focus, with a specific target in sight. Last is influence because in the end, success is about significance, making this world a better place and giving to others through this quest.

As you can see, gutsy is about being "in" (inside, in-grave, insist, inspire, in-choice, in-focus and influence). Open this box, I mean book, and get 'in.' And in so doing, take those steps toward the person we were sent here to be. Find the answers that our hearts have longed for. And tell my mom 'hi' when you see her.

> "Ah, to dream the dream
> And stand in your youth by the starry stream.
>
> Better yet to live life through
> And say at the end, the dream came true."

Inside.

in-side \ in´-sid: an interior or internal part, inward nature, thoughts, or feeling, a light or brilliance stored deep within each person's being.

Key words or phrases: heart, passion, dreams, love, compassion and spirit.

Used in a sentence: *One can only reflect on the outside what is already on the inside.*

"Everyone has inside him a piece of good news. The good news is that you don't know how great you can be! What you can accomplish! And what your potential is!"
Anne Frank

In the late 1950's Bangkok, Thailand, was expanding many roadways in and around the city. One such road project required that a Buddhist Temple and monastery be relocated; a new road would cut it in half. Some of the important statues and paintings from the existing temple would be salvaged and moved to the new temple site. One such item was a ten-foot tall, nearly 3 ton statue of Buddha. The monk in charge of the Buddha statue relocation was nervous. The statue was very old and the centerpiece of the temple.

As straps were put around the statue, the monk looked on. He didn't have a good feeling. The statue was lifted off the ground. "So far so good," he thought; but just then it cracked. The monk's heart sank. "Set it down," he ordered. So, they did. They placed a tarp around it and left it for the day. Later, it began to rain. The monk went out to see if the Buddha statue was staying dry. He lifted the tarp and peered into the darkness. As he did so, his eye caught the crack, and a beam of light returned the glance. Dumbfounded, he left and returned with a sharp tool. Scraping away at the crack, he fell backwards in disbelief. Under the clay figure, was gold!

Blessed is the match consumed in kindling flame.

After the initial shock of such a discovery, the research began. It was discovered that several hundred years ago invaders launched an attack into Thailand. To protect and devalue the gold statue of Buddha, it was covered with clay. These invaders killed everyone by their attack, and the secret died with them. Years later, this mistake led to the discovery that had been hidden for years, a golden Buddha.

We are not much different from this statue. Early in life we knew about ourselves...about the gold on the inside...about our beauty and glory. But over time, the world has given us feedback and beliefs that were intended to 'protect' us. Over time our golden hearts have been covered with mud in the form of pain, hurt, fear, rejection, scarcity. Today this mud is so thick that we have forgotten about our inside, the light and the gold beaming in our core. Don't lose the gold. Consciously scrape these layers away. Rediscover what is inside...and let the gold shine through.

Throw your heart over the bar and your body will follow.
Trapeze artist to his students

Life as a kid is tough enough, but to be a kid that's noticeably different is doubly hard. That's what faced all 5'3" and 80 pounds of Eddie Arcaro in high school. But Eddie was different in more ways than just his small stature; he was also different in the fact that he held a dream on the inside, in his heart. As most of his peers worried about class rings and weekend dates, Eddie's passion for horse racing burned in his heart.

After months of Eddie's cutting class and hanging out at the racetrack his father agreed to allow him to leave school and try his hand at racing. Eddie was so excited; that is, until he tried it. He was awful. Eddie lost his first 100 races. He was clumsy, un-savvy and plain on a horse. Finally the trainer declared, "Send him back to school, he'll never be a rider."

But Eddie's heart told him different. Having lost support from almost everyone in a hundred mile radius, Eddie hit the road. He had nothing except the scares of a hundred lost races and his dream. Was that going to be enough?

He spent months going from track to track. When someone would give him a chance, he would lose his whip, almost fall from the horse, and meet the other horses as they were heading back to the stables as he finished dead last…time after time. Finally after broken bones and hundreds of lost races, one owner took pity on Eddie. He made Eddie his rider win or lose…or in this case lose and lose.

But something began to happen. Eddie began to compete. He learned. It is as if his heart took over…the one that he followed for all of those years. The one that told him, "I can. I can." He began to win…actually he began to win big.

GUTSY (Go Until Time Stops You!)   16

In the next thirty years of racing, Eddie amassed a record that will stand for decades. He won 4,779 races. He is the only jockey to win the coveted Kentucky Derby five times. Eddie Arcaro retired in 1962 at the top of his profession. A millionaire. A legend. But more importantly a person who listened to the inside first... and in the end, he came home.

Tucked neatly somewhere inside each person's heart is a light, a brilliance, a dream –remember? That's the real you and the real me and it is still in there. Getting gutsy is about un-tucking the dream after all of this time. It starts inside. Saddle up, my friends, it's time to ride.

If you're going to be dreaming anyway...dream big!
Donald Trump

"I look at that family, that car, that house and that job; and I think, what a dream..."

I confess that years ago I gazed longingly at luxury cars. I dreamed of owning one, brand didn't matter, I wasn't picky, any one of them would do. I continued living in this dream world until one day I came to a simple yet powerful realization...that at one point in time a luxury car was a dream for the person who now drives it. With few exceptions, he or she didn't always have the skill or education to earn the money to buy that lavish ride. It was a dream for them...one that came to fruition through hard work and focus. I guess one could say that today, they are living in a dream world.

Over time I thought more about 'living a dream world' and bringing dreams to reality, until finally I arrived at a staggering yet unmistakable conclusion that it is all a dream, and we all live in a dream world. In the past I glanced at a Lexus or Mercedes and thought that person is 'living in a dream world.' Over time I have expanded my thoughts to conclude that everything we see, use, consume or have is a result of a dream...let me explain.

The technology in the computer I type on at this very moment was a dream of many scientists years ago. The computer that now sits on my desk was made by a company that just a few short years ago called a garage their world wide cooperate headquarters. What began as a dream of an energetic entrepreneur is now a worldwide fortune 500 company. The parts and assembly for this computer are the careful work of many hands, of people who thought they would probably not be assembling computers for a living.

GUTSY (Go Until Time Stops You!)   18

Yet, this work lets them foster their dreams of providing a nice living for their family, an education, a new television, a daughter's wedding or a car for their teen-ager.

This computer now rests on my desk, one that I dreamed of having in a study that I imagined years ago. I call my study 'the room of knowing.' Its walls are lined with articles I have published, book jackets from books I have written and some awards that I have won, accomplishments I only dreamed of years ago. It is called 'the room of knowing' because I now know I can accomplish my dreams if I set my mind to it. This room reminds me of that. It could also be called the 'room of dreams,' after all, that's where it all started. I guess one could say that as I type, I am working in a dream world, a world of my dreams (the study) and others' (the computer).

As I drive to work this morning, I realize that I can run through the same 'dream drill' with my car. It was made by a company that started small...a dream. Engineers with a vision (or dream) designed it. Workers who are working a dream job because it provides for and creates their dreams assembled it. I can run the same dream drill with the STOP sign at the intersection by my home. It was put there by a crew who dreamed of working outside, in a subdivision that was a dream of a developer, ordered by local, county and state laws, laws passed by people who dreamed of serving their community and country. The sign is in Boone County, Missouri, one of 50 states that make our great country, a country that began in the hopes, hearts and dreams of our forefathers.

I could run through the same dream thought process as I pass the local McDonald's restaurant, my CPA's office, the public library or the state capitol. I could do the same with the water at my tap or the road I drive on or the Green Tea that I quietly sip, but that would be redundant; you get the point. Each and every thing around us is part of a dream that has reached fruition. This reality proves dreams do come true. Anything we touch, have, hold or use is a result of the hopes, energies and imaginations of the ones who created it…it is part of a dream world. Focus on 'a dream world' for just five minutes today and you will realize an appreciation, astonishment and empowerment that you have not felt before…you will literally be opening your eyes, for a first time, in a dream.

"I look at that family, that car, that house and that job and I think, what a dream…"

Look inside and find the call, the voice, the one thing the heart longs for; then take action. Can this dream come true? Yes. Still have doubts? Then open your eyes to witness for the first time…the living dreams that abound.

Look up at the sun's eye and see what the exhalant heart
calls good; that some new day may breed the best because
we gave not what they would but the right twigs for an
eagle's nest.
William Butler Yeats

As most of you know, a car parked in the garage will experience more mechanical problems than one that is driven every day. A ship left in harbor will become un-sea worthy much quicker than one that is sailed on rough seas. A home, not lived in will deteriorate and fall apart quickly. Why do we think our lives are any different? We are made to fly.

It was a fine spring afternoon and a mommy and daddy eagle were beaming over their new baby snuggled in the nest below. They imagined all of the wonderful and terrific things that the baby eagle would do in his lifetime. Late in the afternoon, with the baby asleep, the eagle parents flew down to the river to catch some fish for dinner. As can often happen in the spring, a thunderstorm blew in without notice. Mommy and Daddy eagle had to find cover by the river; baby eagle was alone in the nest.

"Whatever you think you are, you indeed are...but you can fly if you want." The wind blew, the rain fell, and the lightning dashed. The wind blew so hard that the baby eagle was tossed from the nest. He landed on the ground unhurt, fluffed his new feathers and dashed into the underbrush for cover.

The next morning the sun rose and the birds sang as if nothing had happened. A chicken, living on the same farm as these eagles awoke and hopped down from her nest. She headed for the range to peck and scratch. After some time pecking, the chicken noticed a little bird hiding in the underbrush. The chicken, being neighborly, went to the little bird, it was the baby eagle that had been thrown from the nest. She told the baby eagle that he could follow her. She was a chicken and she would teach him to scratch and peck…just like her.

And, that is what happened. The baby eagle, not knowing he was an eagle, went along with the chicken. He learned to peck and scratch and be a chicken. He grew and grew and from time to time he would peer up in the air and see big birds effortlessly floating. He would think to himself, "I wish I could fly." But, he would soon return to reality, after all, for all he knew, he was a chicken.

One day, an eagle flying high peered down. He couldn't believe what he saw so he swooped down for a closer look. There, scratching and acting like a chicken was a grown eagle. The eagle landed and said to the eagle scratching like a chicken, "Hey, don't you know that you're an eagle? You can fly, my friend!"

The eagle acting like a chicken was a little embarrassed; he couldn't fly; after all he was only a chicken. He responded, "No, you must be mistaken, I'm only a chicken. I can only scratch and peck. See." And the eagle showed off his best scratch and peck routine to prove his point. The eagle took off back into the air and shouted over his wings as he left, "Whatever you think you are, you indeed are…but you can fly if you want."

The chicken acting eagle began thinking, "Maybe this eagle was right, maybe I could fly." So, when no chickens were looking, he tried it. He did fly. Not very far and not very well, but he did get off the ground. The next day his wings were sore from the effort but he tried again, better results. He tried again and again until the found that the advice was true, he could fly…after some time he even entertained the notion that maybe, just maybe, he was indeed an eagle.

The chicken acting eagle was eager to tell his chicken friends back at the flock about this new discovery; that he was an eagle and that he could fly. But, to his surprise, they were not happy. They didn't want him to fly. They didn't want him to soar effortlessly high above. They told him to stay down with them, and they called him names like "crazy" and "stupid" and "dreamer" and "foolish." In the end, however, the eagle made the difficult decision to leave his home and friends and be what he was, an eagle.

In this somewhat silly story is found the truth about life. We can fly…the ability is hardwired on our inside. The question is, will we let the inside out and try it? And, will we have the guts to leave the flock that holds us down in exchange for a dream that inspires us to express the beauty, gifts and talent stored within?

Let's not forget who we really are…unfold your wings my friend, we can fly!

"Nothing is as real as a dream. The world can change around you, but your dream will not. Responsibilities need not erase it. Duties need not obscure it. Because the dream is within you, no one can take it away."
Tom Clancy

Natalie was snuggled in close. She was wearing her Cinderella dress-up dress and matching shoes and she and I were once again in the middle of the classic, "Cinderella." This reading was somewhere between the 500 and a millionth time. I lose count how many times we have read this book. But I remember this one very clearly because we were in the middle of the book when it hit me…this book's good.

Not 'good' because a pumpkin is turned into a carriage, although that is pretty neat. It's good because the book is talking about you and me…today…right now. If you don't believe me, do your own research…read it over 500 times in the next two to five years and get back to me. In the mean time let me share what's 'good.'

We were in the middle of Natalie's favorite part…when Cinderella, dressed in the wonderful formal evening gown, arrives at the ball. Since my mind was on cruise control with the words on the page, I drifted while I read and began to wonder what Cinderella must have felt as she danced. It was probably, "Why am I here? I know the invitation said, 'All are invited,' but that didn't mean me. I don't deserve to be here and if I don't leave before the clock strikes midnight, my cover will be blown and everyone will know I am just a poser." Her stomach is in knots as she thinks she doesn't belong yet is having a wonderful time…dancing with some cute hunk; together they seem to be the life of the party.

When the clock strikes midnight for me, it is generally right before I'm to go on stage. It doesn't matter if it's in front of dozens of people or hundreds, I think, "Why do people want to listen to me, what do I have to say anyway; don't they know that a decade and a half ago I was digging ditches and reading meters? Who you fooling run Matt...run!"

And, that's what Cinderella did, she ran. Yet the clothes didn't make the girl...it was what was on the inside. She did belong...it wasn't an act; it wasn't about the outfit nor the clock striking midnight. I realized as Natalie yawned ready for bedtime and I closed the storybook yet again, as the Prince kissed his true love Cinderella, that a part of me tells me to run. To get out, that I am unworthy, unqualified, unfit to live my dream. That part of me is a lie...the dream is the truth. I am worthy as are you...dream, my friend. Show up at your dance and stay...you belong.

I belong. You belong. We belong!

Each time before I walk on stage, I say two things. The first is a prayer, asking that God work through me to deliver a message that will make a difference in the life of at least one person listening. The second thing I tell myself is that I belong.

Nothing is as real as a dream... *There is so much negativism in today's world. This negativism tells us that we are unworthy. The fact is that we are our dream...it doesn't change. The lack, scarcity, fear and unworthy feelings are the lie. We must tell ourselves that we belong...because the simple truth is...we do.*

"Whatever you can do or dream you can begin it," the German author and poet Johann von Goethe once said, "Boldness has genius, power and magic in it."

It is said that President Lincoln would casually stroll down to the Presbyterian Church located on New York Avenue. He liked to go on Wednesday evenings to hear the sermons of Dr. Phinns Gurley. Being the President, he liked to come and go unnoticed; so when Dr. Gurley knew the President was on the way, he would leave the side door unlocked. Through this door was Dr. Gurley's study, adjacent to the sanctuary. President Lincoln could sit it the study with the door just cracked open and hear the sermons.

On one particular night during the walk home, an aide asked the President his opinion of the night's sermon. The President responded thoughtfully, "The content was excellent; he delivered with eloquence. He obviously put thought into the message."

"Then you thought it was an excellent sermon?" questioned the aide.

"No," responded the President.

The aide was confused, "But, Mr. President, you said the content was excellent, it was delivered with eloquence and much work was put into the message."

"Ah, to dream the dream and stand in your youth by the starry stream.

Better yet to live life through and say at the end, the dream came true."
Unknown.

"That's true," the President responded; "but Dr. Gurley forgot the most important ingredient. He forgot to ask us to do something great."

Being great is who we are...

Ever heard the term BHAG? It means big hairy audacious goal; Jim Collins coined it in his best selling book, Good to Great. Sometimes when talking about the inside and dreams, we advance thoughts to goals or better yet BHAGs. Goals are a central aspect of gutsy, but before we set our course (goals), we must peer inward.

In the whisper of a gentle breeze, the black of the darkest night or the stillness of a deep pool, I ask what moves me? Who am I? Why am I here? Who shall I be?

The key isn't what we do but who we are. For it is true, we can only reflect on the outside what we hold true within. The world has sold us on scarcity, lack, fear, pain and mediocrity. Most of us have unknowingly taken this false paradigm hook, line and sinker. In so doing, we reflect it through our actions. Since we get back what we reflect, we are tricked into thinking that we are really these things...and that these things are the truth that is our lives.

But that's not who we are. Inside is gold. On our backs are wings. In our hearts we discover dreams. We belong. Getting gutsy starts inside, with rediscovering the truth about ourselves. And when we do, we reflect greatness, for no other reason than that is who we are.

In-grave.

in-grave \ in-'grāv (*var.* of engrave): to impress deeply leaving a permanent impression or marking.

Key words or phrases: character, values, personal brand and corner of the garden.

Used in a sentence: *In-grave one's values on the soul; for it is nice for others to know who I am but it is crucial that I know.*

*"Act well at the moment, and you have performed
a good action for all eternity."*
Johann Kaspar Lavater

The phone rang; it was Stephanie my wife. Her grandfather was in the hospital again. This time they were asking family to come in; his half-decade long battle with emphysema was coming to an end.

I worked that next day, Friday. We left immediately after work, making the two-and-a-half hour trip to DeSoto Missouri. We immediately went to the hospital bed and said our 'hellos' and prayers with Grandpa. But, after being in car for almost three hours, we found a crowded hospital room was no place for our kids, ages four and two at the time. I mean they liked it. There were lots of neat things to pull and tug on. Dad liked it not so much, however; so I left Stephanie at the hospital to spend time with her dying grandfather and to support her mom. I didn't know for sure where I'd go, just some where away from there; maybe Disney World or swimming (in a Missouri winter) or crazy…most likely though to my brother-in-law's…

Was this hard? Yes. Was this uncomfortable? Yes. Did I want to be doing other stuff with my weekend? You bet! Was I a little upset? Absolutely.

The weekend was fast food, short hospital visits and a dying relative. It was out of place, tired and wild crazy pre-schoolers. It was out of sorts, the 'time is near' and time to eat more fast food. By Sunday afternoon I had the car loaded and was waiting for Stephanie. 'Let's go' was my only thought. 'Let's go now!' It was about this time that the hospital decided to move Grandpa upstairs to the hospice area of the hospital. His life was measured in hours not days.

Stephanie wanted to stay. To support her mom and be with her family through this last hours. I said okay.

Was this hard? Yes. Was this uncomfortable? More than a little. Did I want to be doing other stuff with my weekend? Of course. Was I a little upset? You know the answer to that one.

I drove with the kids back to our home. In my head I was dealing with how I was going to get the kids to school, dressed, and fed in the coming days. How was I going to do Natalie's hair, for example? I took such great care of my own that it fell out. I made arrangements, and lucky for me my mom said she would come over and help out.

Early that Monday morning the phone rang again. Stephanie told me that Grandpa had passed away. She had been there, holding her mom's hand.

She called me later that day with arrangements. The visitation was on Wednesday and the funeral on Thursday. I reminded her that I was scheduled to speak in front of almost 400 people in Springfield, Illinois, that Thursday. And, I planned on doing that instead of attending a funeral…after all, isn't that what Grandpa would want? It was silent for a long time and then she simply replied, "Do what you think is right."

Was this hard? Yes. Was this uncomfortable? Yes. Did I want to speak in front of the audience? Absolutely yes. Was I a little upset? More like a lot upset!

Later that day the fact that I value my family as one of my highest values came to mind; at least I say I value my family. Unfortunately or fortunately, depending on how you look at it, I knew what I needed to do. With less than 72 hours' notice, I called the facilitator of that conference and asked if I could possibly be replaced on the agenda. He understood. I called my boss and asked for two days' vacation for Wednesday and Thursday. I was going to the funeral.

As chance would have it, my daughter's pre-school class had a field trip that Wednesday. So, before going back to DeSoto for the visitation, I was able to go with her and her class on the field trip. I was the only dad there. On Thursday before they closed the casket, I was able to hold my son and say a final prayer for Grandpa. He and I talked about death. It's a moment I won't forget. Stephanie, over this week was able to spend time with many of her aunts, uncles and cousins; she really enjoyed that week.

In the end I was very disappointed that I missed the conference. I was very unhappy, since this was not what I had planned. I was disturbed and otherwise distressed. That being said, however, I wouldn't have changed this choice for the world. I lived my value...and in the end that's all that mattered.

When values are 'in-graved'...decisions are clear...maybe not easy, as it wasn't easy to cancel the speaking event that I worked so hard to get, but the decision was clear. Finding ones core values begins the process toward gutsy because once these values are 'in-graved,' decisions flow freely.

"Not the maker of plans and promises, but rather the one who offers faithful service in small matters. This is the person who is most likely to achieve what is good and lasting."
Johann von Goethe

My grandfather, Otto Forck was a plumber and a good one, too. In the 1950s and 1960s in Jefferson City, Missouri, he owned and operated Otto Forck Plumbing. If you needed something done inside or outside of your home on your plumbing system, you called my grandfather...he knew his shit...no pun intended.

My great grandfather was Henry Forck, who was my father's grandpa. My father still tells stories about Grandpa Henry. Living just two blocks away, my father would walk down to Grandpa Henry's early on warm summer mornings and the two would squirrel hunt up on the old Nelson Farm. When my dad was older, back then being ten or eleven was older, Grandpa Henry would slip dad a piece of tobacco or a sip of beer. I always smile when I read this, we have squirrel hunting, a chew of tobacco and a sip of beer; we are a trailer and a tornado way from a really good country western song.

Being four generations removed from my great grandfather, I'm not ashamed to tell you that he was a sharecropper. He left school at an early age...that's what many boys did back then. He was not educated. By some standards he may have even been illiterate. But, my dad to this day still tells me that he could spell a few words one of which was the word love. Being mostly uneducated, however, he spelled the word a little different; he spelled it T-I-M-E.

You see, it is the love spelled T-I-M-E that Grandpa Henry showed my father and my father's four brothers. He showed love spelled T-I-M-E by telling endless stories on the front porch swing or hunting or fishing or teaching about life and work and fairness and respect. He spelled love a little different; it was spelled T-I-M-E.

There is an old saying, "You can pretend to care, but you can't pretend to be there." With values it's the same; where we spend our time (being there) reflects our values. We can take inventory of our love for ourselves (spelled T-I-M-E) by noting where we spend this time. Is it in front of the television, with our children, spouse or friend, worrying, reading, meditating, exercising, golfing, fishing, helping others, on the Internet, working or pursuing our dream? Our mouths might try to tell one story, but our feet tell the truth.

*"All our dreams can come true, if we have the
courage to pursue them."*
Walt Disney

Terry Fox was an athlete. Actually he was considered one of
the best high school athletes in or around Port Coquitlam,
British Columbia, and won the "Athlete of the Year' award
as a senior in high school. His goal, besides college sports,
was to become a physical education teacher.

In March of 1977 as Terry approached his High School
Graduation he began to be bothered by a pain in his right
knee. After one excruciating
run he finally gave in and
asked his mother to take him to
the doctor…then another. It
was cancer; osteogenic
sarcoma cancer to be exact.
The only treatment at the time
was to amputate the leg.

> *"How many people do
> something they really believe
> in? I just wish people would
> realize that anything's
> possible if they try. Dreams
> are made if people try."*

After losing his leg, Terry had to endure over 15 months of
chemo and radiation therapy. It was during that time that he
decided. He had a dream to turn the pain into gain, to raise
awareness and money for cancer. He set a goal…raise a
dollar for cancer in the name of each person living in
Canada, so that someday another young athlete that hears the
words osteogenic sarcoma cancer won't be faced with losing
a leg or arm or life. It was certain; he would use his one good
leg and make a run for it.

After finishing all cancer treatments and with his doctor's
approval, Terry began training. The plan was that he would
run across Canada. After a year of conditioning, on April
12, 1980, Terry dipped his artificial leg into the Atlantic
Ocean at St. John's, Newfoundland. He looked west and

began what no one had every attempted. His aim was to run a marathon a day, 26.2 miles, until he reached the Pacific Ocean.

It was less than easy. The Canadian Cancer Society supported him as long as there was corporate sponsorship. Terry had sent dozens of letters asking for support. He closed each letter with "...I'm not saying that this will initiate any kind of definitive answer or cure to cancer, but I believe in miracles. I have to." Early on, it was tough going. Motorists would run him off the road. In certain parts of Canada he and his escorts couldn't speak French. They couldn't ask for a meal or shower...at one point they went five days sleeping in the van without showering. But as word spread, so did momentum; things were looking up.

Unfortunately as quickly as they 'looked up,' they were down again. After 143 straight days of running, Terry had to stop. He knew, as only a cancer survivor can, that the pain was not from the over 3,339 miles he had already logged; it was from cancer...it was back. Holding his mother's hand in front of reports he said, "How many people do something they really believe in? I just wish people would realize that anything's possible if you try. Dreams are made if people try." In all, Terry raised over 24 million dollars for cancer...equaling one dollar per resident of the country.

Terry Fox died, with his family beside him, on June 28, 1981. In early fall, the first Terry Fox Run was held in Canada and around the world. Over 300,000 people participated. Today Terry's legacy lives on as the annual Terry Fox Run is held in dozens of countries all around the world. This event is the biggest single-day cancer fundraiser in the world.

When we follow and live our values, pain and hardship dissolve...it is at that point a dream can come true and miracles can happen...

An old proverb reads, "A journey of a thousand miles begins with just one step...take that first step today."

David Morris and Howard Heyer are co-founders of Dillanos Coffee Roasters. What started as a small independent coffee cart in 1991 has grown, to say the least. Today, Dillanos occupies over 26,000 square feet, is approaching $10 million in annual sales and ships coffee all across the United States.

Based in Sumner, Seattle, Dillanos is note worthy not only because of their phenomenal growth, but also because of their values that have led to this transformation. Day to day, Dillanos is guided by their mission statement; it reads, "Help people, make friends, and have fun." Along with this mission statement are their core values. "Possess integrity, honesty and professionalism in everything we do; Provide an extra mile of service, always giving the customer more than they expect; Keep channels of communication open, always focusing on relationships, appreciation and the continuation of a fun atmosphere." They bring life to these principles by having the entire staff recite them together at the end of each staff meeting.

In 1997, one of these friends, a customer in California, was in trouble. *It's a Grind,* at that time, was a collection of four coffee shops based in Long Beach. Because of the UPS strike, David Morris was unsure if he would be able to get *It's a Grind's* order to them. Because of this strike, David had heard that FedEx and the United States Post Office were overwhelmed with volume, and shipments could be greatly delayed. He didn't want his customer, his friend, to be without their beans. Reciting values at the end of a staff meeting is one thing, putting life to a value is yet another. This is exactly what David did. He rented a truck, loaded it with *It's a Grind's* 800 pound coffee order and drove seventeen hours, one way, to deliver the beans. Why? To provide an extra mile of service, always giving the customer more than they expect. And the next week, UPS was still on strike and David made the trip a second time. That's almost 80 total hours in a truck over two weeks for one customer and only a 1600-pound order. Was it worth it?

In life, when push comes to shove, it can be very hard to live values. Often, at the end of the day, or in this case, a long and uncomfortable truck ride, we are left with a lingering question; "Does all of this work ever pay off?" It takes time to measure results. It would have been very easy for David Morris to ask *It's a Grind* to find another coffee supplier instead of spending all of those hours in a truck for such a small order. But, if we consistently live our values it will pay off. In the next six years, *It's a Grind* grew from four stores to over 110 stores in nine states. And, guess who is their exclusive coffee bean provider? It's a small company based in Sumner Seattle, an organization who is willing to live their values.

What do you think of when you hear words like Coca-Cola, Dell, Levis, Harley-Davidson, Apple, Wal-Mart, Nike and Dillanos Coffee Roasters? These are all products with a strong brand name and the mere mention of one of these names congers intense feelings, positive or negative. Dillanos is an example of a strong brand; just ask It's a Grind coffee shops.

What we can't forget is that we each have a personal brand. Successful brands consistently and thoughtfully live their values over long periods of time. What is your brand?

"Every job is a self-portrait of the person who did it.
Autograph your work with excellence."
Anonymous

In the world of sport and competition, arguably, there is no more grueling event, mentally or physically, than a triathlon. Triathlons consist of a 2.4-mile swim, 112-mile bike ride and a 26-mile marathon. Dave Scott was a legend in the sport, winning six consecutive world Iron Man Championships. Dave's success was based on two core beliefs, training and diet.

For me, one who struggles with my three-times-a-week jog around the neighborhood, Dave's training schedule was phenomenal. To prepare and win world Iron Man competitions, Dave would, on average, swim 20,000 meters, bike 75 miles and run 7 miles each day!

With this type of training schedule, Dave could eat whatever he wanted; he was literally burning thousands of calories each day. But he didn't finish a workout like I do, with a half-gallon of Ben and Jerry's ice cream. No, his second core value was the belief in a low fat, high fiber diet. For example, when he ate cottage cheese, he would first put it in a strainer and rinse off all of the fat.

Dave Scott didn't need to rinse the fat from his cottage cheese; after all, he was burning calories by the thousands. But Dave thought that after a long day of competition, under the hot Hawaiian sun, at the world Iron Man, it just might be the little things that pushed him over the finish line before any others. Little things like that extra mile in practice, rinsing the fat from the cottage cheese and staying true to his beliefs.

Is your personal brand one that is late for work, over promised and under delivered, too much time spent jabbering with co-workers around the water cooler, poor attitude, uses sick days like vacation, works an 'eight and skate' unless you have already left early that is...?

Or is your personal brand one that arrives early and stays late, is a team player, under promises and over delivers, see no job as too small or too big, is energetic, eager, willing and hardworking?

There is a gutsy little secret that is simply called 'your corner of the garden.' One will never have 'more garden' in life until the one that has been given has been taken care of over time. It doesn't matter if you are delivering pizzas or delivering goods and services to clients on seven continents. If you take it easy, come in late, look and act sloppy, you are hurting your employer; but mostly you are hurting yourself.

Being the best at your present job (taking care of the garden you have been given) will ensure that you will be given more. If you don't, you won't.

> *Life doesn't show up fully until we show up fully for life.*
> Marianne Williamson

So, back to the original question: what is your personal brand? Your dreams and goals will follow with it.

Decisions are easy when values are clear.
Roy Disney

During a recent seminar, a time management consultant took out a one-gallon glass jar. From under the table he pulled four large stones and placed them in the jar. He then questioned the audience, "Is the jar full?" Most everyone shook their heads, "No way, not full."

He then pulled from under the table a container of gravel. He slowly poured the gravel into the jar. Once the gravel was filled to the top of the jar he asked again, "Is the jar full?" It was a tough audience, most still thought 'no.'

The presenter then produced another container from under the table, this time sand. He was able to pour the sand on top of the gravel and stone. Again he asked, "Is the jar full?" The room was split; some thought it was full while others thought more could be put in.

Then the presenter took the water pitcher from the nearby table and poured water into the jar, right on top the sand, gravel and big rocks. This time when the question was asked the audience agreed, the jar was finally full.

At this point the time management consultant asked, "What's the point." One eager young man on the front row yelled, "We can always find more time in our day if we look…there is time available to us"

"That's a good answer," the presenter responded, "but not correct. After a long pause he said, "The point is that if we don't put the large rocks in first we will never get them in our jar."

The large rocks in the jar represent our character and values. The large stones we have consciously or unconsciously put in the jar trigger our actions which determine our personal brand and ultimately how much garden with which we will be entrusted.

Take inventory of your rocks. If you find a rock that should be in the jar but isn't, you only have one choice, dumping the jar. It's not easy because it makes a huge short-term mess all over the table. Spilling the jar means water, rocks, sand and gravel all over the table. Putting a new rock in the jar means no longer doing certain things while beginning to do others. Certain people won't understand; people who seemed like friends might criticize and fade from your life. So be it...this is building your core, your values...your rocks. This nucleus will sustain one through the sickness, short-term set backs, heartaches and the marathon that is life. Find your rocks...include them in your jar.

Insist.

in-sist \ in-sist' \ v: to be definite, unwavering or steadfast about something intended; to demand or require.

Key words or phrases: determination, resolve, effort, patience and persistence.

Used in a sentence: *Insist so that dreams come true, "Most people miss opportunity," Thomas Edison once said, "because it appears in overalls and looks like work."*

"No lions are ever caught in mousetraps. To catch lions, you must think in terms of lions, not in terms of mice. Your mind is always creating traps of one kind or another, and what you catch depends on the thinking you do. It is your thinking that attracts to you what you receive.

Thomas Dreier

Cliff Young strolled to the registration table and asked if he could participate in the race scheduled to begin early the next morning.

"You'd have to wear running clothes," the young woman behind the registration table responded.

"These are my running clothes," Cliff said, glancing shyly down at this cover-all type work and running outfit.

"What about jogging shoes?" the register questioned, "You will change shoes, won't you?"

"I generally run in these," he again answered as they both peered down at his gumboots.

"Well, there is no reason why you can't register," the woman slowly responded. "The fee is pretty steep though."

Cliff had expected that the cost would be great. He paid it and with that became an official entrant in the 1983 Sydney to Melbourne Ultra Marathon,

By definition, an ultra marathon is anything longer than the traditional twenty-six plus mile marathon. I don't know about you; but when I'm at the gym, my favorite machine is the vending machine. A twenty-six mile marathon would wear me out if I drove it, let alone ran; I can't imagine one that would go farther. And farther the Sydney-Melbourne race went, depending on year and exact course, between 810 and 1100 kilometers.

The next morning Cliff was ready to race, sporting what he was comfortable in, coveralls and gumboots. Since he didn't have any qualifying times from other races to present the registrar, he had to begin at the end of the starting line. The world-class ultra marathoners were at the front of the starting line, the middle-of-the-roaders next, followed by those unranked competitors…Cliff among them. He figured that over a several day race that starting at the end of the starting line would not matter. The starting gun sounded. The crowd began to move, and in mere minutes Cliff lost sight of the world-class runners…they were too far ahead.

This race, run over the course of several days, is generally run in packs. The world-class athletes will stay together and run for about eighteen hours straight. Then stop, rest and sleep for about six hours, doing it all over the next day. Once they are about three to five miles from the finish line, the pace picks up; eventually one runner will out sprint the others to take the ribbon.

And that is what happened in 1983 as well. After several days of running for a dozen and a half hours and sleeping for six, the pack of world-class runners broke out into a sprint. Finally one pulled ahead and crossed the finish line to a cheer of the crowd. He fell to his knees exhausted from the grueling event. As he was greeted by a race official the runner looked up and mustered a few words.

"I thought you guys would have put a ribbon across the finish line," he said as he gasped for breath.

"We did," promptly responded the race official.

"I know I have been running for days, but I still know a ribbon when I see one, and there was no ribbon."

"You didn't finish first."

"That can't be…I was in front of all of the world class group; who beat me?"

"I can't remember his name," said the race official, "some guy with coveralls and gumboots."

And so it was that Cliff Young not only won the 1983 Sydney to Melbourne Ultra Marathon, Cliff Young set a new race record, beating the old mark by nearly two days. You see, Cliff had never participated in a race like this. He didn't know about the run 18, rest 6 rule. Instead he thought it best if he ran 22 hours and rested 2. So, sometime in the dark of the third night, Cliff Young coolly ran past the world-class runners as they slept.

Shortly after the race a reporter asked Cliff how he was feeling.

"Blistered. And stiff."

"In your life, is this the worst you have ever felt?" the reporter questioned.

"Yeah. Worst I've ever felt, yeah."

"Do you think this is the greatest time in your life?"

"Yeah, it is, because I've done something I've always wanted to do. I mean, another year or two I wouldn't be able to run anywhere, you know, I'll be too old."

Cliff Young set an Ultra Marathon record, shattering the old mark by two days...and by the way, in 1983 Cliff Young was 61 years old.

Insisting means running farther, longer and harder than we have ever run before. Even if our outfit (cover-alls and gumboots) doesn't fit the race we are about to begin, take that first step anyway. Insist today, before it's too late.

"An invincible determination can accomplish almost anything and in this lies the great distinction between great men and little men."
Thomas Fuller

The news that Duke University Head Men's Basketball coach Mike Krzyzewski was offered the Los Angeles Lakers Head Coaching job both startled and shocked the Duke Basketball community. In front of their 'very own Duke Coach' in the first week of July 2004 was a five year, forty million dollar contract offer.

So, what does one do when faced with the fear of losing the most successful basketball coach since John Wooden led UCLA? Well, most simply prayed and hoped; chalking what will actually happen up to cosmic fate or 'events out of ones control.' But that wasn't the case for Duke University junior Andrew Humphries. Andrew, a loyal fan since childhood and dedicated Cameron Crazy (that's what they call the student cheering section) since arriving at Duke, was determined to try something. He set to work drafting an email, telling Coach K exactly the reasons he should stay and continue to be 'my coach' as Andrew stated it in the email. "When someone's afraid, they do something to make themselves feel a little empowered." Humphries stated after sending the email.

Coach K. took the weekend to agonizing over the decision; move to LA and coach the Lakers or stay? He and his wife, Mickey, juggled over the pros and cons. At one point, they checked email. There, from a student named Andrew Humphries was a note…Coach K. read it. And, among the tears it brought to his eyes, the decision was clear. He was to stay at Duke. Later that week at the press conference announcing Coach K.'s decision to remain the Duke Head

Basketball coach he said, "If Andrew's listening, thanks a lot."

Andrew enjoyed his fifteen minutes of fame, appearing later that same day on ESPN, talking about the email and the fact that he, possibly saved Duke Basketball. Andrew responded, "I'm not going into the record books or anything but somewhere in there my name is in the mix of things that happened in Duke Basketball."

Really, what, are the chances of a 19 year old kid influencing a $40 million dollar job offer to the best basketball coach of our time? Well, 'small' would be an overstatement but Andrew acted anyway. And, on issues that matter to us, we should too. It doesn't matter if we think our voice will be heard or not. We need to talk, as Coach K. himself stated, "You never know what's read." And, we never know what will make 'the difference.'

Speak out! If a teenager can make a difference in something important to him, in which he seemingly had absolutely no control, think what we can do in our own lives...put your name in the 'mix,' resolve today.

"In the absence of wind," an old sailor's
adage begins, "row."

It was senior day for Notre Dame, the last regular season football game of 1975. There were only twenty-seven seconds remaining on the game clock, and the scoreboard reflected the fact that the game was all but over. In these final moments first year head Coach Dan Devine allowed a few unknown 'practice' players to dart onto the field. With the snap of the ball, one of these practice players, wearing number 45, eluded a blocker and dashed at the quarterback only to miss him and fall face first in the turf.

If Notre Dame had placed names on the back of jerseys in 1975, the name would have read *Ruettiger.* Most of us may have been dejected when our one and only chance to get in the game is met with a face full of turf. But for Ruettiger this was par for the course. He knew exactly what to do. And to understand the whole story, we must understand the many hardships, set backs and roadblocks he overcame in order to even don the jersey. It didn't matter that he was a senior and on the only play he had ever played at Notre Dame, he just missed the quarterback. No, instead Ruettiger hustled back to the huddle; there was time for one more play.

Ruettiger, born in 1948, was the third of 14 children. He carried a small build; and despite his deep love for sports, he had an average athletic ability. After high school, there was no money for him to go on to college. Regardless, his grades weren't good enough for admittance to the one school that he wanted to attend, Notre Dame. So, he quietly tucked his dream of playing college football away and enlisted in the Navy. From there he worked in a power plant. One day a close friend of his was killed on the job. Ruettiger walked away having lost a close buddy and having found a fact in life: That one should measure the obstacles in terms of the

GUTSY (_Go Until Time Stops You!_)

dream. If the dream is big enough, the obstacles can't stack up.

With that in mind, he applied and gained admittance to Holy Cross College. He needed to establish a respectable grade point average in order to even be considered for Notre Dame. Over the next two years he met the struggles in the classroom head on. In fact, it was at Holy Cross that Ruettiger found the reason for his struggles in school; he was diagnosed with Dyslexia. With tutoring and help from teachers, he learned how to study and be effective in the classroom. Finally, after three rejection letters, at the age of 26, Brian Ruettiger was admitted to Notre Dame University.

That of course was only half of the dream; the other half had to do with football. He immediately walked onto the team; but at 5'6" tall and 180 pounds, he was nearly laughed at by the other players. But, once they saw him play…it wasn't the athletic ability; it was the drive to play every down like his last. He played with heart, passion and insistence; that won the respect and admiration of his teammates.

After clearing the grass from the helmet and rejoining the huddle; Ruettiger lined back up for the last play of his college career. As the ball was snapped, he again faked out the blocker; only this time he didn't miss, he sacked the quarterback as time expired. His teammates rushed the field, hoisted Ruettiger to their shoulders and carried him off of the field. As they ceremoniously carried him off, the chant of R-U-D-Y could be heard. You see, Brian Ruettiger's nickname was Rudy.

Insist on your dream or goal. Insist that it comes true. Rudy had no wind…he had to row, every inch of the way. Measure obstacles in terms of the goal; and if the goal is big enough, the obstacles won't stack up.

"Don't fight a problem, solve it!"
Millard Fuller, Founder of Habitat for Humanity

We made the decision, we were moving. We no sooner placed the 'for sale' sign in our yard than we had a contract. That of course was great news...the problem was that the people who were buying our home had to move in three weeks...that now meant we had to move in three weeks, too!

We were able to collect ourselves as well as belongings and get them into a rental house. From there we began the process of looking for our new home. Early on we decided that we would build a house. We contracted with an agent, found a floor plan and agreed on two builders who could bid on the project. Once the numbers were in, we were shocked...the house was tens of thousands more than we expected. Dejected we asked another builder to give a bid...it was in the same price range.

The answer seemed to be clear; it was a loud and resounding 'No!' We were disappointed and parted ways with our real estate agent. A few weeks later we picked out another 'lesser' floor plan and approached another builder. We talked at length on the phone and tentatively agreed on a price...everything seemed to be 'a go.'

As we met this builder on location, however, he began to change his story. The price he had quoted was on another type and style of house and wouldn't apply to the type and style of home we were looking to build. We left it that he would e-mail some plans that were in our price range...we never heard from him again...the answer was still 'no.'

A few weeks went by and I began calling builders again. I called one who owned a lot that I really liked; to be honest, I thought it was way out of our price range. He had just started a home on that lot and asked us if we wanted to meet him to take a look. We agreed to meet.

We were very tired of the rental home by now and ready to give up on the home we 'wanted' and settle on anything. I thought this was probably just a formality because I was sure that this house would either be out of our price range or a style that we didn't like.

We met the builder and talked for almost two hours. The home was very close to the original floor plan we had picked out; only this one featured some upgrades that we didn't think we could afford. The lot was the best we had looked at; it would be a great one for our kids. As for the price…I was floored, it was in our price range…I couldn't believe it.

A week later we agreed on final terms and signed a contract. About five months later we moved into our new home. All along this process, answers kept coming back 'no.' Instead of being thankful for 'no,' I was angry. This process taught me to appreciate 'no.' It means it is not right or this one's not for me. And if I can be patient, there is something even better waiting.

Appreciate 'no' when it comes to your dreams; be it a job, home, book, promotion, vacation, etc. It means for some reason that you are not ready, or conditions are not right. Don't give up, keep after it and be patient. Accept 'no' as a friend. Once you do it will allow you to see a bigger plan for your life, one that will offer perks better than you can ever imagine.

Insist, persist and be patient…

*'The lure of the distant and the difficult is deceptive. The
great opportunity is where you are. "*
John Burroughs

I finally set my bag down on the hotel bed. I plopped next to
it and took a deep breath. *Wow, what a day!* I thought to
myself. Leaving my house at five in the morning, I was
presenting a program to a group of electric utility workers in
St. Louis, Missouri, two hours later. After that I was in a
meeting until noon. Next I sped to Warrenton, Missouri, to
present a safety program to a second group of utility
workers. When that was over, I loaded up my laptop
computer and power point projector and left Warrenton,
driving east on Interstate 70. I crossed the Mississippi River
at 5:30 pm traveling north on I-55, destination, Collinsville,
Illinois.

Arriving at my hotel, I felt great to finally sit down and catch
my breath from the day. Tomorrow, I would be presenting
to a group of natural gas employees in Springfield, Illinois,
before my return home to mid-Missouri.

I glanced at the alarm clock next to the bed; it was six
o'clock (in the evening). I picked up the phone. Stephanie
told me about her day and updated me on the kids. When I
hung up, I decided to drive down the street for a quick
dinner. I wanted to hurry. There was an article that I was
writing, and I wanted to finish it before bed. I knew of a
Mexican restaurant down the way. So, that's what I did.
Taking a book called *Moments of Grace* by Neale Donald
Walsch with me, I went to eat.

I drove to the Mexican Restaurant and found that it was
packed! The parking lot was full and people stood shoulder
to shoulder on the outside patio. I remembered that it was
Cinco de Mayo, but I didn't expect this. *"Too crowded for*

me," I thought. I stopped my vehicle and scanned the skyline for other choices. A block north I spotted a sign for a barbeque joint. *"Sounds good."*

I parked, grabbed my book and went in. I was seated, ordered a diet Pepsi and began to read. I was enjoying myself. It was quiet, only the sound of silverware on a plate, the muffled tone of conversation and an occasional cash register drawer springing open. The waiter returned with the drink; and I ordered the smoked turkey, baked beans and fries and continued to read.

I liked the book. In one section, the author, Neale Donald Walsch, talks about the shameless God. What he means is that God will stop at nothing in His pursuit of us. God will use a bird or billboard sign or a song on the radio or anything to communicate to us, to let us know that He is one with us. Silently I agreed.

My food arrived. I set the book down and folded my hands for a few seconds, something I normally don't do. I took a deep breath, thanked God for the food, the day's presentations, for my family and safe travel. I envisioned success in the next day's presentation.

As I reopened my eyes, I immediately became conscious of the music on the restaurant's overhead speakers. I had not heard this playing since I had stepped foot in the place. At the exact moment, the words from a popular country and western song came to my awareness. I heard, *"Every prayer shall be answered, and every dream shall come true. For right here in this moment is where I'm supposed to be, here with you, here with me."*

Insist, persist and be patient, understanding that 'no' is good and that right where you are in this exact moment is exactly where we need to be to reach our dream. Brian Ruettiger, for example, played college football at age 28; ten years after graduating from high school. To reach his goal, he needed the experience and the resolve gained from it, of serving in the Navy and working in a power plant. Without it we would never have been inspired by a 1993 movie called Rudy. Appreciate the set backs and the answer 'no,' knowing it is exactly what we need to succeed.

"Everyone's got it in him, if he'll only make up his mind and stick at it. None of us is born with a stop-valve on his powers or with a set limit to his capacities. There's no limit possible to the expansion of each one of us."
Charles M. Schwab

Titus Adams was a normal six-year-old boy. Living with his mother and twin sisters (age 2), he loved games, Batman, Lego's and cheese burgers. Titus was normal in every way but one. When the sun went down, Titus was terrified. Darkness for Titus was instant cold sweat, so scared that the body freezes in place, vision goes black and 'Oh God, get me out of here!'

You see, Titus had night terrors. Now night terrors are much more that the typical childhood 'scared of the dark.' Night terrors are a clinically diagnosed fear, one so powerful that a person can't function if exposed to darkness. At age two, Titus' night terrors worsened. And, when the sun goes down, the lights at Titus' home come on and stay one until the sun returns.

On Thanksgiving Day, 2002, Titus and his family enjoyed a great day at the grandparents'. Living just north of Denver, Colorado, -Galeton, Colorado, to be exact -Titus, his mother and sisters made the hour-long trip to Denver to share the holiday with family. It was a great day for everyone. All had plenty of turkey, games and fun. After leftover turkey and mashed potatoes, his mother put the pajamas on the kids and readied them for the hour ride home.

It was on this ride, as they were just minutes from their country home in Galeton, traveling on a dark two-lane blacktop road that the cell phone rang. The phone was in his mother's purse, which was just out of arm's reach, on the passenger floorboard of the truck. Unbuckling her seatbelt, she reached down to get the phone. As she did so, she inadvertently veered off the road. It happened so fast she didn't have time to correct the truck, and they flew into the ditch. They overturned. Titus heard screaming and yells. After three or four rolls the truck stopped.

Titus and his sisters were buckled in. He did a quick survey of himself and the twins and all were okay. He yelled at them to be quiet…finally they settled down. When quiet, Titus could hear a faint sound of a woman's voice…his mother. "Help." It said, "Help."

Telling the twins to 'sit tight,' Titus quickly unbuckled his seat. For a long moment he peered out the broken passenger window. It was dark out there…so dark. Finally he took a deep breath and crawled out the window. He stood planting his bare feet solidly in the several inches of Colorado snow. The wind cut through his pajamas. It was seven degrees.

Terrified in the darkness Titus couldn't move. He could hear the whimpers of his sisters and the faint cry of a lost mother. Though only six years old, Titus had to act. He knew his life hinged on this moment…what to do?

Peering onto the night, Titus saw a light on the hill. He had traveled the road enough to recognize the light as the Galeton Dairy. He also knew that it ran 24 hours a day. So, facing his biggest fear, the darkness, Titus braced himself again the cold and began the walk toward the light. It was so dark that he didn't see the barbed wire fence as it cut his arms and knee. Finally after what seemed like forever, Titus reached the barn.

Help was called. The ambulance transported his mother to a local hospital, but was it too late? There, she vacillated between life and death for three long days. Finally, she pulled through.

Titus Adams literally saved his mother's life. He fought his biggest fear, the darkness, along with the cold and thought of losing his mother to walk a quarter of a mile for help. He wanted it badly enough…to save his mother and sisters. He did what it took. What an example he is for us all!

So, just how badly do we want it anyway…our dreams? Are we willing to do the equivalent of climbing into a cold winter's night, wearing nothing but thin pajamas, plant our feet in the snow and say, "I'm going to get this done"?

The path to gustiness and success is through patient insistence. The only question that lingers is how badly do we want to save our lives? Are we willing to persist until we reach that light at the end of a cold November night?

Inspire.

in-spire \ in-'spī(ə)r \ v: to drive on, impel or motivate; to move to or reside at spirit.

Key words or phrases: to bring out courage, bravery, passion and positive risk taking: to understand 'water-mark.'

Used in a sentence: *To be inspired isn't functioning in the absence of fear; instead it is the ability to move forward despite the fear.*

Blessed is the match consumed in kindling flame.
Blessed is the flame that burns in the heart's secret places.
Blessed is the heart with strength to stop its beating for
honor's sake. Blessed is the match consumed in
kindling flame.
Hanah Senesh

They were given two minutes to turn around and retrace their steps. To return to Brown Chapel A & E church in Selma, Alabama, where the march had started just mere hours earlier. Instead, their leader John Lewis asked the 500 mostly elderly black men and women to kneel and pray. With that John Lewis went to his knees. He later recalled hearing the sound of hoofs advancing on the kneeling mass, the hoofs from the horse of the mounted state police. He recalled hearing the sound of wood clubs against the skulls of people. Then he was hit. The strike put a one-inch gash in his skull…then his memory went black.

The march had begun only a few hours previous, but the events leading up to the march had been a week in the making…centuries and a week really. As John Lewis gave final instructions to the marchers, reminding them to remain calm, not resist or fight or carry anything that could be construed as a weapon, none of the marchers really expected to reach Montgomery…the state capital some fifty miles away…they didn't talk about it, but they could feel it. They began walking in spite of the fact that Alabama Governor George Wallace announced the day earlier that the protest would not be permitted. Jim Clark, the county sheriff, began to deputize any willing and able white man over the age of 21. They marched in silence, not knowing what to expect but expecting the worst.

Their leader, walking in a dark suit and tie covered by a long coat to protect against the sharp March breeze, was John Lewis. John was no stranger to conflict, yet he believed in justice and equality for all people. He subscribed to the Ghandian theory of non violent protest and over the previous half decade had been jailed, beaten, spat upon and ridiculed for his actions. It was to the point that he had been beaten all a man could be beaten…they had beaten the fear out of him. Courage and hope were all that remained.

A week earlier he had led a group of older black folks to the Selma County, Alabama, courthouse. His intention was to register them to vote. On the courthouse steps waiting for Lewis was Sheriff John Kelly. Kelly told Lewis, "Lewis, you are an outside agitator. You are the lowest form of humanity."

"I may be an agitator," Lewis responded. "But I'm no outsider. I was born ninety miles from here and I'm going to stay here until we can register these people to vote." They stayed a week.

For people dedicated to equality this moment, this day, March 7, 1965, will forever be known as Black Sunday. The march was in response to the death of Jimmy Lee, a young man who was shot in the stomach trying to protect his grandfather from being beaten by authorities. He died a few days later. This march was their response. The lines were drawn…it was only a matter of time. Many of the civil rights leaders preferred that the march be cancelled. In the end John Lewis was allowed to lead the march, not representing their organization but on his own…as a person, an individual.

The country was shocked as one of the major television networks broke in on programming late on the afternoon of March 7. There they ran raw footage of the event. The newsreel showed peaceful and well-dressed people kneeling just as they crossed the Edmond-Pettis Bridge. It showed state troopers in white helmets and riot gear advance on the column of people. It showed clubs and cattle prods violently striking people. It showed horses trampling kneeling elderly. It showed John Lewis taking the first blow, a shot to the stomach with a club, then a second to the head. His blood mixed with the blood of those behind him on the cold pavement below…Millions of Americans knelt, too, that night…in shame they echoed a prayer to the heavens.

Ten days later President Lyndon Johnson stood before Congress and said "We shall overcome," and introduced the Equal Right to Vote Act. "At times history and fate meet at a single time and a single place to shape a turning point in man's unending search for freedom," Johnson said.

John Lewis later wrote, "When I care about something, I'm prepared to take the long hard road. That's what faith is all about."

Fear is simply the opportunity to exercise courage, to be inspired. Something inside is ready for courage; ready and willing to 'take the long hard road.' Our history and fate will meet at a single point if we so choose. It's called our dreams…walk with courage for there is nothing that can hurt us here.

"There are a thousand men more qualified for this job, but it is now mine to do and I will do it."
Harry S. Truman

A baby was born on February 12, 1809 in a one-room log cabin on Nolin Creek, in Hardin County, Kentucky. The baby was healthy and grew to be a toddler and then a young boy. When he was eight, his family moved to the backwoods of Indiana. Later, at age nine, the boy was kicked in the head and thought dead...he recovered. Months later his mother fell ill and died.

When he was 21, the family settled in Illinois. In 1832 at the age of 23 years, with only months of formal education, the man decided to run for the Illinois General Assembly, but he lost.

He was part owner in a local village store and lived in the back room of that store. After he lost the election, the store went out of business. He was left badly in debt. Two years later, the store partner died, leaving him with all of the debt, over $1,000.

In 1835 his girl friend, the love of his life, died. She was 22 years old.

In December of the following year, he suffered from severe depression.

In 1837 he proposed marriage to the women he was dating, she said, "No."

In 1940 he was engaged to marry a women named Mary, but secretly liked another women.

In January of 1841, he again suffered from an episode of depression.

He did marry in November of 1842, to the women named Mary.

In 1843 he ran for US congress and lost.

In 1850 his three-year-old child died.

In 1855 he ran for U.S. Senate and lost.

Four years later he again ran for a Senate seat and again was defeated.

Despite all of the professional set-backs and personal pain and suffering, this man never gave up; and in November of 1860 this man, Abraham Lincoln, was elected the 16th president of the United States.

Yet before he took office in March of 1861, President elect Abraham Lincoln was facing a crisis as seven states seceded from the Union. During the train ride from Illinois to Washington, D.C., for his inauguration, there was a failed assassination attempt.

With the start of his Presidency, began the Civil War. The Union thought it would be a quick battle; yet within the first fourteen months of the war, Union forces suffered unbelievable losses at Bull Run, Shiloh (13,000 Union killed or wounded), the Second Battle of Bull Run and Antietam (26,000 combined Union and Confederate dead, wounded or missing). Add to this Lincoln's personal tragedy of the death of his son Willie, age 12 and his wife's emotional breakdown after Willie's death, from which she never fully recovered.

It wasn't uncommon for the President to retire to his bedroom (now the infamous Lincoln bedroom), close and lock the door and remain there for days, suffering from depression. After all, the Southerners hated him. The Northerners didn't like him either, since the war was dragging on. His wife was crazy and his second son was dead. Locked in his bedroom, Lincoln possibly was thinking, "I give up!" Or, "I'm never coming out of this room!" Though overwhelmed and feeling totally inadequate, Lincoln, however didn't remain locked in his room. Instead he faced all of his fears and pains, opened the door and walked forward, leading this great country through the most turbulent time in its history.

And, as he said in his second inaugural address less than 45 days before he was killed, "With malice toward none; with charity for all; with firmness in the right, as God gives us to see the right, let us strive on to finish the work we are in."

I, too, have locked dreams behind the closed door of my heart. I have buried them deep, protecting me from fear, heartbreak, failure, rejection and criticism. But just as Lincoln, we have work to do. Keep our eye on this finish, for failure doesn't exist unless we make it so. We may shoot at the target and miss, but it is only failure if we pin the label. Unlock the door and walk into life.

"There's no scarcity of opportunity to make a living at what you love. There is only a scarcity of resolve to make it happen."
Wayne Dyer

Art Tatum was born in 1909 in Toledo, Ohio. He was born blind in one eye and grew up in a poor family. Growing up, he was picked on by other children and at times beaten by them. It was in one of these fights that he lost sight in his one 'good' eye. Growing up, Art had one desire and passion that seemed completely unachievable. That dream was to play the piano. He had two huge obstacles: one being blind, he couldn't see to play; the other was because his family was poor, they couldn't afford a piano let alone piano lessons.

Still, Art wanted to play so he took every opportunity to learn what he could. He would have a friend or family member walk him to the salons and nightclubs of Toledo, Ohio, in the 1920s. There he would sit and listen. Over time, he would seat himself at the player piano and let his hands feel the keys. At first, it was overwhelming; it seemed that too many keys were moving at the same time. "I can never learn to play," he would think. But he didn't give up. He picked up one note then one chord, then one verse, then one song. Over time Art's desire to play the piano came to fruition. He not only played, he became one of the greatest piano soloists of jazz improvisation.

The interesting thing about Art is the way he learned to play, letting his hands feel the keys on the player piano. What Art didn't know was that when player piano music was made, it was put together using two pianists. Meaning, when you watch a player piano and see the keys move, you are watching four hands play the piano. Art Tatum became the first person ever to learn to play four hands of piano with two hands. No one ever told him he couldn't do it. His passion told him he could…and he did.

When it comes to getting gutsy, live your passion…be inspired! And live, knowing that if you do what you love to do well enough, eventually people will pay you to do it. "Believe in yourself," Cynthia Kersey says; "And there will come a day when others will have no choice but to believe with you, too."

"Conditions are never just right. People who delay action until all factors are favorable do nothing."
William Feather

When the name Christopher Columbus is uttered, I immediately think of sailboats and the ocean blue. But, there is much more to this man born in Genoa, Italy in 1451 than first meets the eye. For starters, Columbus was a visionary. He was able to see past the conventional 'earth is flat' thinking of the time. Through research and other ventures, he formed a new model, one that said that the earth is round. Not only is it round, he formulated that if one would sail west, away from the continental shoreline and directly into the unknown, he would not fall off the edge of the earth. Instead, he would find a better and faster shipping lane to India.

Columbus held this belief and the next step was to prove it. He needed to find some venture capitalists to fund the expedition. In 1484 he talked

If you want guarantees then you don't want life...sail on my friend.

to King John of Portugal and tried to persuade him to buy stock in the "The Enterprise of the Indies." A polite 'no' was the answer. Columbus didn't give up, however, and he moved to Spain in 1485. There he began to learn the language and the culture. In the early 1490's he was able to convince Spain's King Ferdinand and Queen Isabella that his ideas had merit. They offered some financing, Columbus was ecstatic, and he was sailing west, into the unknown.

Columbus assembled a fleet of three relatively small ships and a crew that totaled 120 men. On August 3, 1492, he bid farewell to Spain. He landed on the last known civilized port, the Canary Islands in early September. There he made repairs to his ships and restocked for the journey into the unknown. They set sail into uncharted waters on the morning of September 6, 1492. Can you imagine the mix of exhilaration and anxiety sailing with Columbus and his crew?

Since no one had ever sailed this path, there was no way of knowing just how long it would actually take. After ten days, the crew began to get a little restless. After twenty days, the exhilaration was gone and the nerves were in full throttle. Men held watch, looking for the edge of the earth, just in case their fearless leader was wrong. After thirty days of sailing into the unknown, there was still no sign of land. Finally, after forty long days and dark nights in uncharted ocean, they spotted land.

The rest, of course, is history. But, lost, somewhere in the story of what Columbus discovered and in the crimes he may or may not have committed after landing in the new world, are some ageless truths. Lessons about challenging the status quo; in Columbus' case, the 'earth is flat' thinking. Today that's called, "We don't do that around here." The next lesson is about courage. Columbus literally, "Pulled anchor leaving the shoreline behind; sailing into the unknown." Today that is symbolic of the courage we need in life. Last, keep sailing for forty days, despite those around us that are 'on-watch,' just waiting for us to fall off the end of the world, so they can be the first to say, "I told you so." In our lives that forty days might be ten years or twenty-five years. It stands for that fact that we must keep sailing until we reach our 'new land.'

Let go of the fear that tells us that we will fall off the end of the world. Have the courage to sail, knowing it might take more than 40 days. Getting gutsy is life work. It can mean years and years at sea with 'earth is flat' thinkers all around ready to laugh once we fall. Setting sail (being inspired) means finding a whole new world. If we want guarantees, then we don't want life. Welcome fear, for it allows courage. Welcome fear and life and hoist anchor and sail...

You must experience the immediate pain to avoid the
greater pain farther down the road
Andrew Grove

In 1984, Andrew Grove was a senior vice president of Intel Corporation. The job at that time was not easy. The economy was in a down turn and Intel was turning down with it. The DRAM (DRAM stands for dynamic random access memory, a type of memory chip used in most personal computers) market was flooded; it was time for a change. The financial reports and market analyses over the last few years were confirming this fact to Andrew; he knew it was time to act.

One day he went into his boss's office, the CEO of Intel. They were talking about the down turn and how, in a few months once the stock tanked, they would both be fired by the board of directors, replaced by high priced consultants that would be charged with turning the company around.

That's when the idea hit them...what are the consultants going to say and do? They stepped back and asked, "What would we do if we didn't run this company?" Meaning, if we were outsiders looking in, what would we do to turn this thing around?

The answer seemed obvious at the time: we would get out of the DRAM business completely and move into newer more competitive technologies, probably the newly emerging new microcomputer processor business. Armed with this new realization, Andrew Grove and Intel's CEO led the board of directors behind closed-door meetings. The bleak reality of the 1984

Change, live and endure the short-term pain of tomorrow's success.

market was again explained along with a new plan...a new vision of tomorrow.

In the end, as you probably already realize, that's what they did. They stopped making the DRAM and began making the microprocessor. It wasn't easy. In turning the corner, they were faced with the challenges such as potential lay offs of hundreds of trusted and trained employees, building new production lines and training the work force in this new product and having to borrow the money to do it.

In the end, it was the right move. The company endured the short-term pain of change and now is the world's largest chipmaker, also a leading manufacturer of computer, networking and communications products.

In the midst of the final writings of this section, Nathan, my four- year-old son, was taking swimming lessons. Last summer we swam almost everyday, and he got very comfortable in the water. Since that was nearly ten months ago, he is again apprehensive about the water. In his swimming lessons he would do everything the instructor asked except let go of the side. It didn't matter that he could touch the bottom of the pool...he was afraid to let go. And, it's hard to swim while holding the side.

For some of us, our obituary will read, "Born 1962, died 1987, buried 2046." In the middle of life we sometimes find ourselves in the pain of making a decision, of letting go of the past and starting anew. We know that we are really asking, "If I weren't in charge of myself, what would I do?" Or "Can I let go of the side of the pool and swim?" Often, despite all of the 'market signals' or assurance from the lifeguard that things will be okay, we just can't let go. And in time...we die.

Change, live, find passion and inspiration and endure the short-term pain of tomorrow's success.

"Ships will deteriorate and rust quicker when left at dock and not sailed. A home will fall apart rapidly if abandoned and not lived in, for ships are made to sail and homes to be lived in. And life...to be lived."

A major high-end hotel chain empowers and encourages each and every employee, from the housekeeper to the bellhops, to assist customers in need. After the appropriate training courses, these housekeepers, bellhops and hotel staff are each given a discretionary account that can be used in order to help a customer. If the customer forgot a pair of shoes, for example, this hotel chain empowers line employees to go purchase a new pair. Don't ask the boss, just please the customer. And, how much money is placed in each discretionary account to assist customers? With no questions asked, any line employee can assist a hotel customer up to $2,000. Yeah, that's not a typo, it's two grand!

This hotel chain, along with many other businesses and companies, uses the watermark principle to empower employees to make decisions and take chances. To picture this principle, envision a ship floating in water. Some of the ship will obviously be out of the water, above the watermark and some of the ship will be below the water. When taking a chance, one should ask, "If I act and miss, will that make a hole in the ship above the watermark or below it?"

If it's a mistake but it hits above the watermark, it was a risk worth taking; the ship can sail on. But, if one tries

Behold the turtle...he makes progress only when sticking out his neck.

and fails on a mark below the water line, the ship (business or company) will sink. This hotel has decided that everything up to $2,000 is considered above the watermark. If an employee is going to spend more than that to help a customer, he should ask his boss.

Find the watermarks in life and take the risks...how important is risk to success? Read on...

Risk the least, live the least.
If we want guarantees then we don't want life…

My life changed forever in the spring of 1977. I will never forget the words my mom uttered across the kitchen table on that Saturday morning. She uttered, "Summer school."

That was thirty years ago and why did kids go to summer school? Today there are enrichment programs for children, and many go to school year-round, but back then one went to summer school for one reason and one reason only. They were failing and about to be held back. And specific to me, I was failing reading.

I should have seen this whole summer school thing coming. I mean if your parents go to a PTA meeting in disguise; it might be a sign. But how was I to know? I was in second grade, a mere seven years old, how was I to know that there aren't costume parties in March?

I would like to tell you that something great happened to me that summer. I would like to tell you that I was able to get on par with my peers from the summer of study. I'd like to report that I made some great friends and had some great teachers. I remember one thing and one thing only from summer school, and that is, if I was good, which means I sat still and listened, for two straight weeks, I earned a free soda. Now, my family was poor in the summer of 1977 and we didn't buy soda, so if all I had to do was sit still and listen to get a free one, I was in. I mean I may have had a slight learning delay but I was no dummy.

We would get our sodas every other Friday along with an hour of playtime on the playground. On this particular Friday however, it was raining. So, we were going to have our sodas in the gym. The big kids, ages 13 and 14, were already in the gym, had chugged down their sodas and were playing dodge ball. The instruction to us 'little kids' was to get your soda and line up against the wall. You know what they call that today, lawsuit.

Anyway, I was next in line for my soda and my mouth was watering. I couldn't wait to take a drink. I got to choose between Coke, Dr. Pepper, orange or Sprite, but my favorite of the day was grape! I took the soda from the table then took two steps. As I turned to walk over to take my place against the wall, I had one of those 'life stands still moments.' There, a foot from the most important thing in my life, the grape soda, was a big red dodge ball. It was coming at a high rate of speed and was going to rip that soda right from my hands. Then the split second was over and what had been a loud, noisy, playful gym was immediately quiet. The sound of the glass bottle shattering on the cold tile floor penetrated their noise and left them standing still. And, guess who they were looking at?

It was so quiet in the gym as the entire Thorpe Gordon elementary summer school student body starred at me, I could hear the fizz of the soda upon that hard tile floor. I could feel the soda through the holes in my blue Converse tennis shoes. And, in front of the entire student body, a teacher approached and began, in no uncertain terms, to tell me how stupid I was for dropping my grape soda! To be honest, this scared me. This is the part that I am embarrassed to admit. What do you think I did right on top of the grape soda, as the entire student body watched, in the summer of 1977, as this teacher berated me? What did I do?

Were you thinking that I wet my pants? If so, you are sick and need professional help! I cried. All of the frustrations of a learning problem; all of the frustrations of a poor family; all came out in front of the entire school on that Friday afternoon. I cried for what seemed like ten years but it was probably only about ten seconds. Then I saw, through my tears, another teacher approaching. She was wearing a sundress and a smile and I'll never forget what she did. She knelt down and gave me a hug. She said, "Matt, I saw the whole thing, you didn't drop the soda, the ball took it from your hand. Take this soda and go sit with your class. It's not your fault."

And, as the dodge ball game resumed and the janitor worked to clean up the soda, those words, "It's not your fault," echoed in my head. The learning problem was due to conductive hearing loss when I was two and three years old. If one can't hear at those critical ages then the speech is messed up, if the speech is messed up then it's hard to read because the phonics are messed up. That wasn't my fault. The condition at home wasn't my fault. I was a mere seven years and at this tender age had done little to contribute to the problems that I was born into. I realized, as I dried my tears that this teacher, while giving me only a few kind words and a grape soda, literally saved my life. And I realize, looking back some thirty years removed, that she took a big risk to do so. The teacher that berated me was a senior teacher, much older than the one who helped me. This younger teacher took a risk. She stepped out to go against a peer and in so doing, saved my life.

Studies have shown that success is dependant on one key quality; the ability to take positive and healthy risk. This young teacher took a huge risk to approach me as one of her peers berated me. We too need to take healthy risks to improve our lives and the lives of others. Remember, risk the least, live the least. If we want guarantees then we don't want life...Risk is a vital part of being gutsy. Let go of the side of the pool and swim...for failure only exists if we make it so.

In-choice.

in-choice \ in 'chòis: to move, live or reside at choice. To select or decide with care.

Key words or phrases: positive attitude, non-victim, thanks-giver, life script.

Used in a sentence: *Maybe Victor Frankel, Holocaust survivor, defined the concept of 'in-choice' best when he said, "Everything can be taken from a man but one thing, the last of the human freedoms, to choose one's attitude in any given set of circumstances; to choose one's own way."*

Whether you believe you can or believe you can't,
you are generally correct.
Unknown

One of my earliest memories as a child is of my mom
shaking me, waking me and pulling me from bed very early
one particular morning. She, along with my Dad and two
sisters got in the car; it was still dark and we drove to a large
field just outside of town. As the sun was making the horizon
orange, large elephants began work, hoisting a tent. The
circus was in town. My family watched from one of dozens
of cars as the dawn broke and elephants, obedient to their
masters, worked to raise the big top.

What I didn't know then but have since learned is how
elephants are trained. For circuses and cultures that still use
elephants for heavy labor, this training begins when the
elephant is still small, less than 250 pounds. Using a fairly
strong rope, the animal will be tied to a large tree, concrete
post or otherwise unmovable object. There, the young
elephant will be left to pull, tug and gnaw, all in an attempt
to break free. But over time, after even more pulling,
yanking and gnawing, it will give up…its spirit broken.

It is at this point when the strong rope can be removed,
replaced with a small one. The massive tree isn't needed
either, a small stake will due. Once an elephant has learned
that it can't break the rope it will never try again. The owner
can then secure the animal, whether still 250 pounds or a full
grown, four-ton elephant with
a small rope stake. It won't
break free, for the elephant
believes that it can't.

*At any point in time we
may choose in favor of
ourselves…*

Remembering back to those elephants, that circus tent, I
remember how powerful they were. What they could move,

lift, build. And, I wonder too, how much more power they might have if they realized they can't be held down. There is no stake with their name on it...they are free.

Where are our stakes...what do we *believe* holds us down?

Reaction and creation have the same eight letters yet are polar opposites. Reaction is being strapped to a garden stake. We could decide differently, only we don't think we can. Creation is deciding that there are no stakes, no ropes that tie us down. Decide with care, and in so doing, create the world around...

Even chance events that seem to be minor when they occur can have effects far out of proportion to their initial importance.

Ever heard of the Butterfly Effect? Technically it is known as Sensitive Dependence on Initial Conditions. By definition it simply says that the state or condition of a complex system, over time, depends on its initial conditions. It's called the Butterfly Effect because the following story is used to explain this phenomenon. The *Butterfly Effect* suggests that even the tiny changes in air currents created by a butterfly flapping its wings in Peking China today, create a series of magnified results that can change the weather across the globe, transform a storm system next month in New York, for example.

The theory grew from the work of Edward Lorenz and is now known to have some validity, especially with weather prediction. In 1961, Lorenz discovered that his computer gave him a different answer when he started at the beginning of his calculations than when he took a "short-cut" and started near the midpoint. Actually it should not have mattered, because the differences were so very small they should have been negligible. But the final result, he discovered, was highly dependent on the starting conditions.

The practical conclusion from Lorenz's work was that long-range weather forecasting is doomed to failure. This is not because we can't measure well enough; in fact the radar, weather models and technology used for weather forecasting are very accurate. The problem is that the air currents created by the flap of a butterfly's wing under certain conditions can create a series of magnified results to the extent that it can literally affect the weather across the globe. It's the flap of the wing and other similar conditions that can't be predicted.

These short verses by an unknown author go a long way to help explain The Butterfly Effect (Sensitive Dependence on Initial Conditions):

> For want of a nail, the shoe was lost.
> For want of a shoe, the horse was lost.
> For want of a horse, the rider was lost.
> For want of a rider, the battle was lost.
> For want of a battle, the kingdom was lost.

In life, be "at cause" not effect. Being "at cause" might mean that we are tiny butterflies in a large world; but even if that's the case, it is strongly suggested that butterflies can literally change the world. Be at cause...choose wisely!

"The hardest arithmetic to master is that which enables us to count our blessings. "
Eric Hoffer

Late yesterday afternoon I stared aimlessly out the window into the dark drizzle of a cold Missouri November (2004). In three days, Thanksgiving will be celebrated all across this great country, but what in the hell do I have to be thankful for? After all, my beloved Missouri Tiger Football team is playing like Thanksgiving turkeys instead of a once top twenty-ranked football team with a Heisman hopeful. The St. Louis Rams are playing like Christmas yams. Boston is still World Series Champs; I still can't believe that one. If that's not enough, I'll be bunking in a hotel this Thanksgiving weekend, since my in-laws moved to Omaha (of all places). To top it off, a few hours earlier I found out that this cough I have had for the last three weeks is bronchitis. I'm staring out the window because my mind's blank. I have an article to write for my weekly newsletter and all I can think of is I haven't seen the sun in weeks.

It was at that moment I had a great thought; write the article tomorrow. After all, tomorrow is the greatest labor saving device ever invented. With that I turned the computer off and vowed that upon waking tomorrow morning, for one hour, I would take detailed notice of each and everything that I am thankful for. I was sure the list would be short!

So this morning the alarm rang and I remembered my promise; for this first hour, I will note all that I am thankful for. I immediately realized I could breathe I am granted another day on this earth. After all, any day above ground is worthy of thanks. I arose from a warm bed with soft sheets and set my feet down on nice warm carpet. I walked into the bathroom and turned on the lights -one third of the people living today don't have electricity. I turned on the shower -

thanks for indoor plumbing, water, hot water to be exact. Soap. Shampoo, although I don't need nearly as much shampoo now as I once did. I have a nice clean towel and nice clean clothes. I am blessed with toothpaste, a toothbrush and teeth, for that matter

I left the bedroom and walked into the kitchen. I pulled a container of Soy milk from a refrigerator that is full of food. I poured a glass and remembered a statistic I heard on the radio recently: 12% of the United States population goes hungry each day. I grabbed a banana and realized how lucky I am to be able to walk down my stairs and to be able to see where I am walking. I sat quietly and watched the gas log fireplace flicker as dawn crept through the windows. I gave thanks for the natural gas that fueled the fire, the ceiling fan above that circulated the air and the rocking chair with soft cushions in which I sat.

As time passed, I heard a voice; it was Natalie, my four-year-old daughter. She joined me, resting on my lap. As the sun rose, Nathan, my two-year-old joined Natalie and me. What a blessing! Eventually, I had to leave; after all, I am blessed with a job, not only a job but a great job. I kiss the kids and their mother, leaving them to a warm house and cartoons. Thank God for TVs. Preparing for the road, I slipped on a nice pair of shoes, filled my lunch box with food, poured fresh orange juice into a cup and filled a zip-lock with Cheerios. I stepped into the garage. I am lucky to have a garage and even luckier to have a nice vehicle to park in it.

I sit now at my desk, ninety minutes into my day, and I am struck with wonder and awe of the blessings that are before me each day: simple things like carpet, sheets, soap and teeth. I realize that often I am not a thanks giver, instead a thanks-for-nothing type, not realizing what blessings are in my life. Yesterday I was a thanks-taker, taking for granted

GUTSY (Go Until Time Stops You!)

health, happiness, success of a college football team and life in general. I was a thanks-wanter, wanting my in-laws to be back in the same old town or wanting the sun to shine. I have been a thanks-whiner, complaining about trivial day-to-day things. Last, I was a thanks-timer, thinking I would always have time. But, in this last hour I realize that I must have an attitude of gratitude. I need to realize all of the things in my life that there are to be thankful for and that I have been blessed with. And, in so doing, I will be a true thanks-giver.

What we send out is exactly what we get back. Spending time each day in sheer appreciation of all that has been given to us will not only brighten our day...it will come back to us to stay.

"A great attitude does much more than turn on the lights in our worlds; it seems to magically connect us to all sorts of serendipitous opportunities that were somehow absent before the change."
Earl Nightingale

A retired man was repairing his motorcycle on his patio in Florida while his wife was busy in the kitchen. The man was racing the motorcycle engine when, somehow, it slipped into gear. Still holding on to the handlebars, the man was dragged through a glass patio door and dumped onto the floor.

Hearing the loud crash, the wife came running. Through the glass and motorcycle exhaust she found her beloved husband lying on the floor next to the motorcycle. He was cut and bleeding with shattered glass from the patio door throughout the room. She ran to the phone and called 911. Living on a fairly large hill, the husband suggested that she go down, the several flights of stairs to the street, to direct the paramedics. That would probably speed things up. After the ambulance arrived, the man was transported to the hospital. Since he was doing okay, the wife returned home to begin the clean up. She up-righted the motorcycle and wheeled it back outside. She swept up the glass and noticed some gas on the linoleum floor that had leaked from the gas tank. She wiped it up with paper towels and threw them in the toilet.

Meanwhile, at the hospital, the husband was treated and released. He hailed a cab for the ride home. Upon returning home, he looked at the shattered patio door and the damage to his motorcycle. He was very upset and went to the bathroom, sat on the toilet and smoked a cigarette. After finishing the smoke, he flipped it between his legs into the toilet, of course he was still seated.

The wife, who was in the kitchen heard a loud explosion and ran to find her husband lying this time in the bathroom. His trousers had been blown away and he was suffering burns on his buttock, the back of his legs and groin.

The wife again called for an ambulance. The same ambulance crew that had responded hours earlier arrived again at the home. As they carried the man on a stretcher down the long flights of stairs to the street, one of them asked how this could have happened. Once the wife told them, one of the paramedics laughed so hard that he dropped his corner of the stretcher. The man fell down the remaining stairs breaking his arm. (Unknown).

And...you think you're having a bad day...

Getting down is not a problem; it happens to everyone. The problem is staying down. In the words of the great motivator Zig Ziglar, "One doesn't drown by falling in water, one drowns by staying down in the water."

Get up! Decide how long you will stay down and then get up. Gutsy is about making the choice to get up, time and time again...

*"A dream is just a dream. A goal is a dream
with a plan and a deadline."*
Harvey Mackay

You awaken and immediately decide it's going to be a great day, or you decide that it's not.

You drive to work and the car next to you suddenly cuts you off. You can choose to immediately respond with understanding or with anger.

You get to work and your boss tells you about a change in operations that will happen next week. You can choose to be excited about the opportunity or fearful of the change.

Later in the day, you are asked to lunch by a couple of new guys from another department. You can decide to make new friends and go or be small and kindly decline.

*The hidden secret of life,
however, is that we are
a product of the simple
decisions we make each
moment.*

Before you leave for the day, you receive an e-mail about giving to an annual charity campaign. You can choose to give freely or hold on tightly.

When you get home, your toddler asks you to play 'batman and monsters.' You can make the choice to join in the fun or refuse.

At dinner, the dog jumps on your lap again -who let the dog in anyway? You can choose to be patient and calmly let the dog outside, or you can show your frustration and fatigue.

After dinner, your oldest child brings in his math test; he earned a 'B.' You can choose to encourage and recognize the effort or tear him down by asking why it wasn't an 'A.'

When you go to work in your shop later in the evening, you can choose to wear safety gear, or you can make the choice not to wear it.

At bedtime, as you turn off the light, you can choose to tell your spouse what he/she means to you or you can keep quiet.

What kind of day would it have been if you had chosen the former in all cases? What type of day would it have been if you had decided on the latter in all situations? In these cases there are not any 'rights' or 'wrongs' just simple choices. The hidden secret of life, however, is that we are a product of the simple decisions we make each moment. Each day we make hundreds if not thousands of choices. We make a conscious choice for happiness, leadership, a smile, love, kindness or generosity. Or we just as easily opt for smallness, fear, anger, resentment, bitterness or hatred.

So, what type of day is it? The choice is up to you.

"We either make ourselves happy or miserable." Carlos Castaneda says, "The amount of work is the same." Sometimes we don't want the responsibility for our lives. We won't admit we play in our happiness or misery. It's called victim. Being gutsy starts with the simple concept of choice and ends when at the end of the day we realize that each and every action was of choice. Happy or miserable? Dealer's choice.

Life is 2% what happens to us and 98% how we react to it.
Attitude, it can make or break.
Unknown.

I gave a presentation relating to safety sometime back. After the meeting I hung around and talked to people one on one. I like the individual setting for heart-to-heart conversations, and I had many that morning. After several minutes the crowd began to break and shortly it was just this other guy and I in the room. As our eyes met, he said that he had a safety concern. I told him to let me hear it, and boy, did he!

He launched a three-minute assault on how bad things were. It was all doom and gloom, the sky was falling, supervision didn't care, equipment didn't work, tools were broken and the water tasted bad. He concluded that his attitude was in the toilet. A bad attitude is a safety concern he surmised because how is a man to work safely when he is in such a sour state of mind?

By nature I think I am a fairly sympathetic person, and my response even surprised me somewhat as I blurted the first thing that came to mind, "You know," I started, "attitude is a choice."

Now, if you really want to tick someone off, remind him that attitude is a choice after he has just invited you to his pity party. He was furious. He glared at me for a second or two then stomped to the door. As he opened it to leave, he fired a parting shot, "I'd like to see you handle this!" And with that, he was gone.

He obviously wanted the last word. He must have forgotten that I write…a lot, so for the whole world to read…this is the "official" last word! Last 'words' really, since there are two of them.

First, attitude is a choice. What more can be said?

Second, don't get caught up in the lie that we try to tell ourselves. It's the one that goes, 'I have it bad and that guy over there has it good.' This is a lie because one person doesn't have it better or worse than any other person. Having it good or bad is a state of being; it is in the inside of each of us.

As humans, we are all very similar inside. Our internal stuff, those emotions and fears, are mostly the same. While each person has a different set of life circumstances, these circumstances do not equate to happiness, success, sadness or defeat. Those are choices.

We can all think of kids from wealthy families that both turned out well and others that didn't. Why didn't they all turn out well? From the outside they seemed to have it all? We all know kids from abusive and addictive homes that turned out well and others that didn't. Why didn't all of these kids fail; shouldn't they have? We all know individuals that have had traumatic life experiences. Some of these people have gone on to live full lives despite what happened to them and others have not.

While people are the same inside, the only difference between success and contentment, failure and misery is that the successful ones at some point realize they get to choose. The first choice realized is attitude.

The ones that do not remember they can choose fall into a dark place with no choices; it's called being victim. It is dangerous ground because once a victim we think that we are powerless. We think that we have no choice and that our circumstances are controlled by force, beyond our control;

by the world or one's spouse or boss or tools that are broken and trucks that don't run. Victims have simply forgotten that they can choose and in so doing, change. We each have that power.

Don't give your power away...

"There's no scarcity of opportunity to make a living at what you love. There is only a scarcity of resolve to make it happen."
Wayne Dryer

Mary sat at her kitchen table with her head in her hands. It was so easy to look back at the hardships in her life. Years ago her first husband had simply walked away, leaving her with

She could literally write the way her life would go. The pen was in her hand and the paper, a new sheet. It was her choice.

three small children. She, at that time, didn't even have a job. She worked hard to provide, even working her way near the top of a company. As men she had trained began being promoted over her, she quickly realized that women in the late 1950's did indeed hit glass ceilings. With the support of her second husband, she quit this job and invested her life savings of $5,000 in a new business venture. In this new business, she would run the field operations and her husband the financials. Two weeks before the product line was to be delivered, Mary's second husband suffered a heart attack while eating breakfast at their home and died.

A week later at this same table, she thought about how unfair it all is. How unfair life is along with all of the hardships and tragedies and work and the loss that comes with it. She knew it wouldn't be easy, but she also realized that this moment (just as in every moment) she had a choice. She could literally write the way her life would go. The pen was in her hand and the paper, a new sheet. It was her choice.

What Mary was writing was her life story and we all have one. There is an old saying by an unknown author, "The best way to predict the future is to create it." A life story or life script develops from the moment we take our first breath. In childhood and through our teens, our life story is mostly written for us by the attitudes and habits and actions that are impressed upon us. Then, all of the sudden we are all grown up. At this point most of us do not take the time to think about all of these thoughts, notions, prejudices or ideas that others have given us over the last twenty years. Instead, these thoughts and ideas are garnered as fact about ourselves or life…you know, "That's just the way it is."

We don't realize that we are in control of our story. Things like 'I can't speak in front of a group' or 'medium income is all I will become' or 'I will never advance in the company past this point' or 'I can never live on that side of town' or 'I don't like that type of music' or even, 'you don't have to live in California to drink soy milk.' We hold these life teachings to be true, without question. But, our life story can be changed. We have the ability to take whiteout and delete beliefs and habits that no longer serve us…to remove things about us we don't like simply to write in new ones. It is our choice; it is our story.

Mary realized her life story as she had written it didn't allow for her to run a successful business without her husband. She was scared. Her three children, now all adults, encouraged her to move forward and start the business. To literally rewrite her life story with a the following: 'I can build a successful business without my husband. I can do it.'

Mary did move ahead with her business and she did okay, too. Her initial $5,000 investment in 1963 is now a $2.5 billion a year cosmetic retailer. By the way, you may know her not by Mary, but as Mary Kay.

Leave behind all of the old thoughts, prejudices and fears that no longer serve you. Listen to your heart to find the real you, the path that is you, your real life script.

It's exciting really...being in-choice. To realize that we not only have some effect on our world, we actually can have as much effect as we choose -up to and including writing our own life story about how we want our lives to go...Cut free, give thanks, be at cause and write the first chapter today. If not today then when...if not you, then who? Remember, the best way to predict the future is to create it.

In-focus.

In-focus \ in-'fō-kəs: concentration, resolve and clarity for a fixed point, direction.

Key words or phrases: goals, vision, mission, limitlessness.

Used in a sentence: *Thomas Edison described being in-focus like this, "The first requisite for success is the ability to apply your physical and mental energies to one problem incessantly without growing weary."*

People today complain about lack of time, but it's not lack of time that is a problem; it is lack of direction.

Zig Ziglar

In sporting events and competitions we play to win, and, the only thing better than a single win is a winning streak. We all have our favorite winning streaks; the Miami Dolphins in the 1970's, the Chicago Bears of the 1930's, Michael Jordan and his six championship rings or the 2002 Oakland A's who won 20 straight games. And, don't forget the most dominant sports figure ever, Howard Hill.

Howard who? Yeah, you know...Howard Hill. He won 281 consecutive archery competitions spanning decades from the 1920's to the 1950's. Actually, no single person ever dominated a sport so completely as Howard did archery. He was never beaten in competition. I repeat, never beaten in competition!

Born on November 13, 1899, in Wilsonville, Alabama, Howard loved to hunt and spend time in the woods. Each time he went out as a kid, his long bow was in hand. By the time he was ten years old, he was spending much time practicing archery. Over the years, Howard not only dominated the sport of archery, he became a master and world-renowned hunter killing elephants, lions and leopards all with a long bow. Howard still holds records for largest lynx, moose, mountain sheep, mountain goat and alligator ever taken with a bow and arrow. He could literally hit the target with an arrow and then split that arrow with a second.

In your mind's eye picture Howard Hill shooting a bow and arrow. Then picture how successful he would be if he tried to hit his target blindfolded. He would still obviously have the same talent. He would be holding the same tools (bow and arrow), and he would be the same guy that invested hours in practice and hard work. Yet, blindfolded, he would have no idea where the target was located or what it even looked like. Blindfolded, he would literally be shooting aimlessly trying to hit something, anything.

So, how can we hit a target we can't see? We can't! And working without a target makes one very ineffective. Each of us blindfolded, for example, would be just as effective with a bow and arrow as the blindfolded world champion Howard Hill. Take the blindfold off and find your target. Set goals and make sure your energies are taking you toward those goals. Your energies once focused are sure to, in time, lead you to the bull's eye...ready, aim...fire!

Focus. You have the talent and the tools. It's possible the only thing missing is the clear target?

There is no passion to be found playing small and settling for a life that is less than the one you are capable of living.
Nelson Mandela

A man wrote the following letter to his insurance company:

Dear Sirs,

I am writing in response to your request for additional information. In block number 3 of the accident reporting form, I put "poor planning" as the cause of my accident. You said in your letter that I should explain more fully, and I trust that the following details will be sufficient:

I am a bricklayer by trade. On the day of the accident, I was working alone on the roof of a new six-story building. When I completed my work, I discovered that I had about 500 pounds of brick left over. Rather than carry the bricks down by hand, I decided to lower them in a barrel by using a pulley which fortunately was attached to the side of the building, at the sixth floor.

Securing the rope at ground level, I went up to the roof, swung the barrel out, and loaded the bricks into it. Then I went back to the ground and untied the rope, holding it tightly to insure a slow descent of the 500 pounds of bricks. You will note in block 11 eleven of the accident reporting form that I weigh 135 pounds.

Because of my surprise at being jerked off the ground so suddenly, I lost my presence of mind and forgot to let go of the rope. Needless to say, I proceeded at a rather rapid rate up the side of the building.

In the vicinity of the third floor, I met the barrel coming down. This explains the fractured skull and broken collarbone.

Slowed only slightly, I continued my rapid ascent, not stopping until the fingers on my right hand were two-knuckles deep into the pulley.

Fortunately, by this time, I had regained my presence of mind and was able to hold tightly to the rope despite the pain.

At approximately the same time, however, the barrel of bricks hit the

The three 'p's' that cause a slow death to millions each year: paralysis, procrastination and purposelessness.

ground and the bottom fell out of the barrel. Devoid of the weight of the bricks, the barrel now weighed approximately fifty pounds.

I refer you again to my weight in block number 11. As you might imagine, I began a rapid descent down the side of the building.

In the vicinity of the third floor I met the barrel coming up. This accounts for the two fractured ankles and the lacerations of my legs and lower body.

The encounter with the barrel slowed me enough to lessen my injuries when I fell onto the pile of bricks. Fortunately, only three vertebrae were cracked.

I am sorry to report, however, that as I lay there on the bricks, in pain, unable to stand, and watching the empty barrel six stories above me, I again lost my presence of mind….and let go of the rope…(*Unknown*).

Being a safety professional, I have used this piece with workers many times to explain the value of planning work. Many injuries and even deaths occur each year because of the dreaded p's...particularly poor planning. But there is another set of p's that cause a slow death to millions each year; these three are paralysis, procrastination and purposelessness.

Get in-focus about where life should go. Find purpose then a plan that begins with the purpose in mind. Without it we are just going through the habit of life...putting bricks in a barrel and when it's full, untying the rope and hanging on for the ride...

You can only have in life what you think is possible.
Unknown

Did you know that there is actually a rock, paper, scissors International World Championship? Yeah, that's right, the game also known as Roshambo, that is most often played to decide who gets the front seat of the car or the last piece of pizza, is also a competitive sport. The 2003 World Roshambo Champion is Rob Krueger. He cut, smashed or covered the competition on the way to the gold medal and the $5,000 first place purse.

The game we played growing up is mostly the same as the world championship except that the game we played would be called a 'lightning round.' Competitors for the world title square off in a best of series. It's something really; there are coaches, strategies, the scouting of opponents, even personal trainers to keep the athletes in shape (okay I was kidding about the personal trainers). There are actual referees with striped shirts that rule over the match and declare the winner. Competitors begin play on the count of four, not three. There are official moves such as an avalanche, which is when a player pitches three rocks in a row.

You can feel the intensity of this competition in Rob Krueger's post championship press conference. He stepped to the podium with the 2003 Rock, Paper, Scissors gold medal and a smile and said, "Marc (the runner-up) and I kept stalemating in the final match, which created a lot of tension on stage. I had to block out the noise of the crowd and concentrate on reading Marc's face. When he threw two rocks in a row, I guessed he was going to complete the Avalanche gambit with a third rock, so I switched strategies at the last second to take the World Championship."

I wonder sometimes if we don't treat our jobs, health, friends, goals, ambitions and life as casually as we play a lightning round of Roshambo? Without much thought we sleepwalk through yet another day of this existence. We treat our loved ones, co-workers and fellow humans as if we are playing for the last slice of pizza...you know...whatever. But our life isn't won or lost with one 'best of series.' We must suit up to play each day, just ask Rob Krueger...Don't let the scissors cut your life, I mean paper, short...now, on the count of four, let's go out and live.

"If you always put limits on everything you do, physical or anything else, it will spread into your work and into your life. There are no limits. There are only plateaus, and you must not stay there; you must go beyond them."
Bruce Lee

Being 'grandma' was a role that Laura Schultz really liked. In the summer of 1977, Laura was 63 years young and enjoyed every minute of it with her grandchildren. On this particular day, her kindergarten-aged grandson was playing in the yard with neighborhood locals. Laura was washing dishes. It was a beautiful day in Tallahassee, Florida. The windows were open, allowing the light breeze to warm her face. She could hear the laugher of the children outside the window.

Suddenly, she heard a terrible scream from outside. Dropping the dishes she had in her hand, she ran out to find her grandson trapped under the back tire of her Buick. She quickly realized that one of the children had crawled into the car and put it in gear. The heavy car rolled backward and now pinned her grandson to the concrete. Fear raced in his eyes, and he screamed frantically for grandma to help.

Laura looked up and down the car. She didn't know what to do. Finally, without thinking, she grabbed the back corner of the Buick and lifted. The tire came off the ground enough for her grandson to slide out. He was unhurt...the two hugged.

Now, grandma can't just lift a car in front of the entire neighborhood children and nothing be said. Instead, the 'fence-row gossip chain' was on fire. In less than two hours some men from the neighborhood strolled to the Buick and tried to lift it...they couldn't. A local

"What else is out there that was impossible but now is in my reach?

paper got wind and came out to do a short piece on the event...*Grandma Lifts Car*...

It was this newspaper article that somehow found its way to Charles Garfield. For years, Charles had studied people in their prime, people who pushed their bodies and/or minds to extremes and accomplished incredible things, from great scientists to Olympic athletes. When he saw Laura's story, he knew he had to interview her. He called her and to his surprise found she didn't want to talk about 'the event.' He tried again some time later, same results. As time moved forward, he found himself in Tallahassee for a conference' and during a break he drove to Laura's house. Reluctantly, she let him in, asking if he might be hungry. She didn't want to talk about 'it' but was being hospitable to someone that had gone to much trouble just to talk to her.

After some small talk, Charles confronted her asking why she didn't want to discuss 'the event.' Laura responded, "When you are my age and you do something that you never thought possible," she said speaking softly while blankly staring out the window, "what else is out there that was impossible but now in my reach?"

Charles asked, "What else did you want to do?"

Laura went on to explain that she had always liked geology. She had planned to go to school, but she met her husband, they had children and the rest is history. "Now," she reasoned, "it's too late. If I go to school now, when I graduate in four years, I'll be 67 years old."

Charles thanked her for the conversation and the snack. And upon leaving said, "You know, Laura, whether you go back to school or not, in four years you will still be 67."

Two years later, Charles got a note in the mail. It was from Laura. She was proud to tell him that she had graduated from a community college with an associate degree. Two years after that, he received another note...she had earned a college degree in geology.

What is possible in life? Bruce Lee's quote is one of my favorite ones, "If you always put limits on everything you do, physical or anything else. It will spread into your work and into your life. There are no limits. There are only plateaus, and you must not stay there; you must go beyond them." Back to the original question, what is possible in life? I'm not sure. I do know it's more than we can ever imagine!

"Success," Robert Collier wrote, "is the sum of small efforts repeated day in and day out."

It might be hard to imagine today, but fifteen years ago…okay twenty years ago…I was a decent high school basketball player. I established two goals between my sophomore and junior seasons. The first was to get my 6'1" frame high enough in the air to dunk the basketball and second to be our team's most valuable player.

To say that my junior season was a disappointment would be an understatement. Hampered by a bad left knee, I opted to forgo surgery until the season was over and play. The result was a knee that was too weak to go. It made for inconsistency and bench time. But, after the season in which I recovered and regained my strength, I refocused my determination and went to work.

In time, I achieved both goals. I could dunk the basketball. If I had at least three steps to the basket, I could consistently 'put it down' with one or two hands. And, when the season was over, my name was called at the winter sports banquet when the MVP trophy was awarded. Yet, fifteen…okay twenty…years later I see a serious flaw in my thinking…one that today can really change my life if I apply it…if I can only be like Mike.

Growing up in Thorp, Wisconsin, population 1,657, Mike thought he could be about as good at football as any farm raised kid from small town America. An NFL leader he would not be, but maybe with luck he could play college ball and that is what he worked toward, college football. After all-state honors as a high school player, Mike did play football at the next level, at the Division III college of Wisconsin, La Crosse. It was after achieving this goal that he set a new one…NFL player.

He began by measuring his achievements, workouts and competition, not against Division III college players but against NFL players. In 1997 after college he walked into the San Diego Chargers training camp...they cut him. He played in the Arena Football League and NFL Europe until the Kansas City Chiefs signed him as a long snapper in 1999. With his foot in the door, he began pushing for a special team spot (those are the players that cover kickoffs and punts). Then he worked even harder; he wanted playing time as a back-up linebacker.

Finally, an injury led to a starting role at the linebacker position, and Mike has never looked back. In 2002 Mike Maslowski, an undersized and slow (by linebacker standards) football player, set the Chief's single season tackle record, a mark which had stood since 1979.

In retrospect of my high school sports career, I am very proud that I set goals and achieved them. But with almost fifteen years, okay twenty years, to reflect, I can clearly see that if I had wanted to play college ball I could have. First I would have had to establish the goal, then measure all of my skill development, workouts, conditioning, summer camps and weight training, not against local high school talent but against the local college talent. In the end, we really never know what limits we have set on ourselves by setting closed end goals. What might seem like a high and lofty endeavor might in fact be too short sighted. Just ask Mike.

Today, knowing I need to be like Mike, I challenge my thinking on goals. When I set limits, I challenge them. When I make projections, I push them farther. I think Donald Trump, a man that knows something about setting big hairy goals, said it best in his recent book entitled *Think Like a Billionaire*. "If you are intent on big success, think big, stay focused, be paranoid (keep your guard up), be passionate, don't ever give up, love what you are doing." In other words, 'be like Mike.'

Think you can...set a goal but keep it open ended...what is ahead in life is bigger, greater and better than one could ever imagine. If you don't believe me then just ask a farm kid from Wisconsin.

Just because they have...doesn't mean you have to...
Just because they are...doesn't mean you are...

Have you ever witnessed a paper airplane contest? Well, neither had I until this February. At halftime of a local college women's basketball game, the athletic department sponsored such a deal. The promotion aimed to improve attendance stated that the contestant who threw a paper airplane closest to half court would win five hundred dollars. So, at half time of the game, anyone wanting to showcase his or her paper airplane talents lined up on the hardwood basketball floor.

Each individual was handed an eight and a half by eleven piece of paper. Over a hundred people twisted and formed the white sheets of paper. The older ones tried to remember back to childhood and all of those paper airplanes of youth. The young ones repeated the one that they had made in class last Friday when the teacher had her back turned. Each stepped up and threw. The line went fast. One right after another, the single file line shortened. The two thousand fans watched, cheering when an airplane slid close to the center court bull's eye. As the line dwindled, no one was really that close. It seemed that there were two throwing styles, the dart style and the 'rear back and let go' baseball style. Each had good points and bad. The dart style enabled the airplane to glide straight, but it did not have enough momentum to carry it to center court. The baseball style toss gave the plane plenty of distance to hit target but no steering. Contestants trying this throw had no control over where the plane went.

Right down to the last contestant, the bull's eye sat wide open. The last participant happened to be a young gentleman, about twelve. He wore faded jeans and a gray university sweatshirt. He stood nervously at the line gazing towards the bull's eye. Then, I noticed something unusual; he had yet to make an airplane. The paper, unfolded, dangled in his shaking hands. He eyed the target some fifty feet away. Suddenly he wadded his paper into a ball, reached back as far as he could and hurled. The crowd erupted as the paper wad sailed across the floor and landed almost directly in the center of the bull's eye. The crowd cheered intensely. The boy jumped up and down. The officials sponsoring the program all huddled, probably thinking, "What do we do now? Was this a legal paper airplane?"

Two days later I thumbed through the newspaper. On the second page of the sports section appeared a picture of a twelve-year-old boy sporting a gray sweatshirt and a large smile. In his hands rested a check for five hundred dollars. Behind Jeremy Weber stood his parents and the college assistant athletic director. A short article under the picture read as follows:

"Amid controversy, Jeremy Weber, son of Donald and Mary Weber, won the five hundred dollar paper airplane toss contest at half time of the women's college game. There was a question as to whether the ball Jeremy wadded his paper into constituted a paper airplane. After deliberation and a review of the rule sheet, contest officials determined that this paper wad could be considered an airplane. Nancy Schneider, assistant athletic director explained that the rules only said that an airplane had to be formed of paper and thrown. The rules did not state any other parameters for the making of a proper airplane. According to the rules, this was a legal airplane. Jeremy was just exceptionally creative, she stated. Jeremy said, with a smile, he knew he needed a new style after watching everyone else's airplane fly and not come close (to the bull's eye). We say, "Nice going Jeremy. You just revolutionized the paper airplane."

There is no doubt that being gutsy will demand creativity and innovation. Creativity is like a row of dominoes; once the first one is pushed over, they all will fall. This means that when we have ideas, push them into the world...that's the only way to get new and better ones.

When I gave my first presentation, it was the best (and only I might add) idea I had at the time. I pushed it forward, however. Today I have several canned presentations that are much better, so much so I use only one small piece of that first one. Had I never tried the first idea, I would not have what I have today.

In writing, when I published that first article, it was the only idea for a publishable piece I had. After that, the floodgates opened, and I have published dozens of articles and written four books.

Do things differently after all we are each unique. Be in-focus on that one idea then move it forward into this world...push over that domino and more will follow.

"Far away there in the sunshine are my highest aspirations. I may not reach them, but I can look up and see their beauty, believe in them, and try to follow where they lead."
Louisa May Alcott

Phaedra Fleming needed a prom dress, without it there would be no prom for her. Phaedra is eighteen now, and reaching the legal age of adulthood means no more foster care. She is still in school and lives in an apartment with the aid of a small stipend from the state of Florida. Phaedra had made up her mind that she wasn't going to the Prom until she talked to her caseworker, Gary Levine and he directed her to Becca's Closet.

Becca's Closet is a federally certified charity that touches countless teenage women each year. For those that can't afford a prom dress, Becca's closet will give them one, a nice designer dress, too. Each dress represents an opportunity that they would not otherwise have. Becca's Closet wasn't always a nationally recognized organization with chapters from New York to California. It literally started with a teenager, Rebecca Kirtman, a vision and her closet.

> *We can choose the best version of our highest vision for ourselves; it is our choice.*

Rebecca loved dresses and helping people. She wanted all girls in or around south Florida to have the opportunity to attend prom—if they needed a dress, she would help. So, she made the conscious decision to collect dresses and give them away to those in need. With a warm and friendly smile, she would help any girl pick out a dress from the more than 250 that she had worked hard to collect.

On August 20, 2003, Rebecca Kirtman was driving home from her high school orientation, as her junior year would begin in only a few weeks. Her car collided with another and Rebecca was killed. She was 16 years old...but her spirit lives. Friends and family in need to make sense of her life and tragic death turned her will to give and her 250 prom dresses into the national charity. They named it Becca's Closet. Today, Becca's Closet is filled with over 3,000 dresses and chapters all across the country. Dress donations have arrived from the TV show 'Days of our Lives' as well as cash donations, the single largest being $10,000 from an anonymous donor from Mississippi.

Rebecca's spirit lives, not only in her charity and those that benefit from it but in the lesson she teaches. Rebecca Kirtman had an idea. She made the conscious choice to act upon it; and in so doing, she chose the best version of her highest vision for herself. Our time is short; each day we have a choice; may we all have Becca's courage.

What an example, a teenager who wanted to help! She was gutsy, and in-focus. She had concentration, resolve and clarity for a fixed point. That enabled her to be that best version of her highest vision. Thanks, Becca! For while your work here on earth continues to help thousands of high-school women attend prom, your example does so much more. It helps each of us be our best version of our highest vision...and that's the highest gift of all.

Influence.

in-flu-ence \ in-,flu-ən(t)s: radiate spiritual or moral force by guiding or producing an effect without a direct exertion.

Key words or phrases: impact, giving, leaving this world a better place, 'it's bigger than yourself,'

Used in a sentence: *In order to have real and lasting influence in this world, radiating spiritual and moral force, live the words of Ghandhi, "Be the change you want in this world."*

Death tugs at my ear and says, "Live, I am coming."
Oliver Wendell Holmes

On a peaceful and unusually cool early August evening in Kirksville, Missouri, I found myself mostly alone on my front porch. Mostly alone, because it was just the dog and I. Now I have never been a canine lover until my wife took pity on this black and white retriever coonhound mix puppy at the local animal shelter. The dog is full-grown and a handful of a hound. The animal and I have spent considerable time bonding since Stephanie went back to college to work on her master's degree. In fact, we are alone because she had to run to the library to find a book for a class.

Together and alone on this quiet evening, we patiently watched people walk by the house, people taking advantage of such a fine evening to exercise. After an hour of watching walkers, I could tell the dog was restless, so I decided, why not? We set out. She and I, walking. We had not gone far when nature called; not for me but for man's best friend. She pooped. I was embarrassed. It was no small deal either, a big dog a big...well, you get the picture. Not traveling with a poop-o-scoop, I had no choice but to stick my tail between my legs and walk on.

> *Swimming in the gray of life with my head barely above water, I seldom give much thought to my "dead-line" except to hope that I cannot yet see it. But I will...*

As we continued our leisurely jaunt, we happened upon a cemetery. It is one that I had not visited since college. While in college, I made several midnight tours of this cemetery because of the legendary chair tombstone. Legend holds that a very rich man died very unhappy. In his after life he made a deal with the devil that he could exchange his soul for the soul of the person that sat on his marker. In order to lure poor unknowing souls, he made his tombstone a chair. I hadn't seen the chair in over five years or in the daylight, so the evening being present, I decided to visit the past. Besides, it may seem morbid, but I enjoy an occasional cemetery visit. Maybe enjoy is the wrong word; I enjoy thinking about life, and no better place to ponder life than at the stopping place. It's reflective. I entered.

On the way to the back of the cemetery, searching for the chair, I realized things I had not noticed on my previous visits. I found one tombstone that read above the name and date, "AT REST." What a grand thought, to have sucked life out of this existence, to have labored and fought and struggled, to have fought the good fight and have run the race, to be tired and now at rest.

Another polished granite marker surrounded by the tall green August grass read, "ROXY, we love you; mom, dad, Scott and Joe." The front read "Roxanne Catherine Miner. 1960-1978." She was eighteen.

I found a section of small, mostly grass-covered markers with the names of babies -babies that had died at birth or shortly after. One lived three days and the one next to it, three months. I pictured the empty baby's room that parents returned to after they left this exact spot where I was now standing. I envisioned a mom and dad returning to the emptiness of home and broken dreams. Thinking. Crying. Asking why? For a moment I felt a fraction of the pain they must have felt and now years latter, maybe still do. I prayed they were given abundant life. Again.

I found the legendary chair. I looked at it and wondered. I did not sit the times before and I did not sit now.

On the way out of the yard, I found a fresh grave. It was the only one in the cemetery, which was good I thought. I stood there with my dog and remembered some of the lives I have watched go. The faces. The memories. The laughter. A life remembered never dies, you know.

The dog and I left. Quietly. The same way we entered; the dog of course unaffected, and I of course continuing to ponder life. The great thread that weaves us all together is that of death. Swimming in the gray of life with my head barely above water, I seldom give much thought to my "dead-line" except to hope that I cannot yet see it. But I will…like everyone I visited tonight. I walked on.

I write to you now over a decade later. If I close my eyes, I can still feel the power of my walk as if it were yesterday. I can still smell the deep green August grass and the moist darkness of the mounded dirt blanketing the new casket. In my mind's eye I can still see the chair. I can feel the pain, the joy and the rest. The last thing you may be interested in about the walk is what I did when I got back home. The matter of the dog's calling card on the neighbor's yard echoed in my head. I realized if I leave stuff lying around for me or someone else to step in, it can get messy. With the darkness of night-fall approaching, I took my poop-o-scoop shovel and cleaned up the mess…I need to take care of my stuff. The walk reminded me of that…and still does.

Clean up our messes and get gutsy…the clock ticks for us all…tick tock, tick tock…

"Whether or not we realize it, each of us has within us the ability to set some kind of example for people. Knowing this, would you rather be known for being the one who encouraged others, or the one who inadvertently discouraged those around you?"
Josh Hinds

The Ancient Romans loved to design and create. Many of their projects have stood the test of time and are still with us today. Examples of such great works would be the Coliseum (built by Titus in 80 A.D.), the Hippodrome (built for horse and chariot racing, able to hold up to a quarter of a million people), the Pantheon and Forum. There are two trademarks of these buildings and of Roman architecture in general, they are columns and arches.

The arches were both beautiful and an engineering marvel. The Romans were able to divert the enormous weight of the arch down to the arch's foundation. During construction wooden braces and scaffolding would hold the weight. After the keystone was finally placed in the arch, the support bracing could be removed. A tradition in Rome was to have the engineer in charge of the project stand under the arch as the bracing was removed. If the design was poor or if he failed in construction…he'd be the first to know.

I wonder sometimes if we would want our children to follow our path? To stand under the arch we have built when we are gone?

What was revolutionary about an arch was that it was a doorway or opening that could replace the post and lintel. Whether using an arch or the post and lentil, these openings were used to support a larger structure, a building, for example. Influence is the last step in being gutsy, and it begins with a simple question about what we are building on earth. Are we leaving an opening through which our thoughts or actions can support the larger structure that will come after our death...that will add to this world, leaving it a better place...allowing others to build on top of our work...that in the end is what life, gutsy and influence are about, and it's the final piece to success...

We make a living by what we get.
We make a life by what we give.
Winston Churchill

Imagine waking up one beautiful morning, opening the paper and reading one's own obituary. That's exactly what Alfred did in 1888. His brother Luduig had passed away, and the paper, by mistake, printed Alfred's obituary. The headline read, "The Merchant of Death is Dead."

To understand this headline, one must understand Alfred and his life. As a boy, he was always interested in explosives. His father, a self-taught engineer and chemist, helped his son experiment with this passion. As a young adult, Alfred studied chemistry both in Europe and the United States, learning all he could about chemicals and how they reacted. In the early 1860's Alfred opened a company that made nitroglycerin. Three years later, he applied for a patent for something he called, the blasting cap. Nitroglycerin was very unstable, and in 1866 Alfred discovered the he could turn nitroglycerine into a dough-like state which could be kneaded. He called it dynamite.

"Every charitable act is a stepping stone toward heaven."

After that discovery, Alfred opened companies that made explosives both in Europe and in the United States. Twenty years later, when he read about his life and death in the paper, he was reported to be an extremely wealthy man. He was a man who had sold his product to governments and countries at war. However, he was a man, who through his life's work had been dedicated to death.

Since Alfred was a very private man, it is unknown the impact that reading of his obituary had on his remaining

GUTSY (Go Until Time Stops You!)

eight years on earth. It is widely speculated, however, that it had a profoundly positive effect. Alfred didn't want to leave a legacy of death. He didn't want his influence here on earth to be that of war, explosion and blasting caps. So he changed that legacy and decided to leave something positive here on earth, something that would have a lasting 'good.' That is why, if asked who invented dynamite, few can answer. If asked what annual recognition for peace is awarded by a foundation along with a cash prize to the one world leader who had the greatest impact on peace in a given year, most know that as the Nobel peace prize. It was established by Alfred Nobel upon his death, inspired by his desire to leave this earth a better place.

To work toward positive influence and leave this world a better place, we don't have to establish an annual peace prize or scholarship foundation or charity. I mean, we can...that's good. But "Every charitable act," Henry Ward Beecher once said, "is a stepping stone toward heaven." Heaven is made each day by the little things we do. And being gutsy through influence can be gained by each small act. I think these simple eight lines by an unknown author say it best:

> Can I say in passing as the day is passing fast,
> That I helped a single person of the many that I passed?
>
> Is a soul rejoicing over what I did or said;
> Is one whose hopes had faded now with courage looks ahead?
>
> Did I use this day wisely; was it well or petty spent?
> Did I leave a trail of tenderness or the scorn of discontent?
>
> Tonight as I lay my head down I hope God will say
> That I helped another by what I did today.

As we lay our heads down for the final time, what will our obituary read? This final step in being gutsy is about leaving this place in better shape than we found it.

"A great attitude does much more than turn on the lights in our worlds; it seems to magically connect us to all sorts of serendipitous opportunities that were somehow absent before the change."
Earl Nightingale

In the 1700s there were only three basic forms of transportation: foot, horse or ship. Shipping to an island or coastline location was literally their lifeline both for supplies and for communication. Scotland was dependent on such a lifeline to survive; yet many of the coastlines around that country were notorious for shipwrecks. With no light to guide the way, nightfall and fog would lead hundreds of ships to ground each year. These wrecks cost the local economies great amounts of money; but more costly were the lives lost, thousands each year, due to shipwrecks.

"We cannot hold a torch to light another's path without brightening our own."

Robert Stevenson was an engineer and a good one. He had an idea to prevent shipwrecks and in so doing save the crew and the cargo. He took his ideas to the government and suggested that lighthouses be constructed so that ships could navigate in dark times, at night and in the fog.

In 1786 Robert Stevenson's ideas and hard work came to fruition as Scotland established the Northern Lighthouse Trust. Robert was named chief engineer in charge of building these lighthouses.

The task wasn't easy. First Robert had to design a structure capable of beaming light miles into the darkness in order to warn of danger. This structure had to be firm and well built, too. It had to withstand gale force ocean winds and pounding rain and still be able to shine its light. Next, the locations where these lighthouses would be constructed had to be accessed, for between the men and material stood hills, great rocks and mountains.

The project was a success and over two centuries four generations of Stevensons have passed the torch as chief engineer for the Northern Lights Trust. Each fought local landowner opposition, government restraints, wind and rain and weather in order to shine a beam of light, a ray that shone so bright that over the decades it has literally saved thousands of lives.

Influence, a radiating spiritual or moral force, is about letting our light shine out to others, to help light their way. And, in so doing, "We cannot hold a torch to light another's path without brightening our own." (Quote from Ben Sweetland)

"Good timber does not grow with ease; the stronger the wind, the stronger the trees."
J. Willard Marriott; Founder of Marriott Hotels

What does it take for us to stay home from work? Some days it seems like the threat of a cold, or the perception of the possibility of a mild ache, might be enough to keep us home. But what if in the course of 'getting to the office' there had been 30 assassination attempts on your life, would you still come in? If, within the last year, your house had been hit with mortar shells, machine gun fire and hand grenades all in an attempt to keep you at home, would you still come in? If you had to travel with US Marine escort, hire 50 bodyguards for your home and have two platoons of troops keep vigilant watch around your office, would you still come in? If, your child had been kidnapped so that you would resign, would you still come in? If the three people who held this job ahead of you had all quit or been killed would you still come into the office each day?

This is exactly what Maamoun Sami Rashid al-Awani, the governor of Anbar providence Iraq, has faced since being elected to office last January (2005). What keeps him going is the knowledge of how important the job is. Of Iraq's eighteen providences, the most violent remains Anbar, home to the city of Ramadi, population 1.6 million. Saddam Hussein drew his top-level intelligence and military officers from this region, which is the second largest city in the country (behind Bagdad's six million people). With the close ties to Saddam, the insurgents, those who want both al-Awani out of office and the United States out of the region, are strong.

But al-Awani won't waver; even though his armed motorcade must drive a new route each day, to protect against planned roadside bombs. And, despite the fact that

GUTSY (Go Until Time Stops You!)   132

once at his office, he must dash from the vehicle to the building under the protection of armed Marines, to protect from snipers, he comes in each day. Other government council members have not had this level of commitment. Of the original 40 elected, only about two-dozen show up regularly. If they do show up they will find al-Awani at his desk...he comes in.

He draws his courage from an American leader, President John F. Kennedy. His favorite quote, "Ask not what your country can do for you, ask what you can do for your country." About the hazards of the job, he simply says, "There's nothing greater than serving my country."

For governor al-Awani, his passion for change and a free country does not waver. It stands strong through gunfire, assassination attempts, assaults on his home and even the kidnapping of his child (who was returned unhurt after a ransom was paid). He is determined, not just some days, not just on Tuesday afternoons and Friday mornings, he is determined to come in each day. Rain or shine, gunfire or bombings...it means that much.

During a hurricane in 2005, the military members assigned the duty of guarding the Tomb of the Unknown Soldier were given permission to stand down and suspend the assignment. They respectfully declined the offer, "No way, Sir!" Soaked to the skin, marching in the pounding rain of a tropical storm, they said, "Guarding the Tomb was not just an assignment, it is the highest honor that can be afforded to a serviceperson."

Influence, being committee to something greater than oneself like the Soldiers at the tomb of the Unknown Soldier or Maamoun Sami Rashid al-Awani, is the highest honor that we can pay to ourselves and to our countries. When we succeed we not only prove 'it can be done' to ourselves, we prove it to the world...for all who watch. Decline the offer to sit and watch TV, give up, eat chips and grow lazy. Though the wind might blow and obstacles will be put in our path, move forward toward influence. For it is not just an assignment...it's the highest honor afforded to a person.

*"Do all the good you can, by all the means you can, in all the
ways you can, in all the places you can, at all the times you
can, to all the people you can, as long as ever you can."*
John Wesley

Recently, a short excerpt in USA Today caught my eye. It
talked about a young 33-year-old woman named Jamie
Howard and her battle with cancer. The article talked about
how she has just undergone a double mastectomy and
chemotherapy and radiation treatments. Doctors say that her
prognosis is good for a full and healthy life. That would not
have been the case a few years ago. In fact, doctors estimate
8.9 million people are alive today solely because of advances
in cancer research. Of the people who have been diagnosed
with cancer in the last 30 years, the five-year survival rate
has risen from 38 percent to 59 percent.

Reading that article took me back a few years. I remembered
former college basketball coach and television broadcaster
Jimmy Valvano and recalled the story that Duke University
Head Basketball Coach Mike Krzyzewski (Coach K) told in
his book, *Leading with Heart*. Jimmy Valvano and Coach K
were close friends. They began coaching in the same college
basketball conference together, the Atlantic Coast
Conference, years earlier. In the summer of 1992, Jimmy
Valvano was diagnosed with cancer; and less than a year
later, the spring of 1993, he lay dying in a hospital bed at
Duke University Medical Center, Durham, North Carolina.
There his good friend, Coach K, visited him daily.

It was during one of these visits, Coach K later recalled, that
Mike was extremely upset. He asked his family to leave the
room and Coach K to close the door.

Once the door was closed, Jimmy opened up to Coach K.
"Mike," he began, "I have done it all wrong. All of the wins,

the 1983 National championship, the success as a TV commentator...I did it all for me and now, as I'm dying I realize that I need to be a part of something greater than myself...I need to leave something here..."

"You're not dead yet," Coach K encouraged.

With tears in his eyes, Jimmy said, "You're right, and I have been doing a lot of research on cancer. Only about 15 percent of all cancer research grants submitted to the U.S. government are funded. That leaves some really good research undone because of a lack of funding. I want to start a foundation that funds some of this research."

So that's what Jimmy V did from a wheel chair during his last days on earth; he spoke and lobbied to start a foundation to fund cancer research. In one speech he said, "We need your help. I need your help...it may save someone you love."

Jimmy Valvano lost his battle with cancer on April 28, 1993, but his work done from a hospital bed lives on. To date, the Jimmy V Foundation has raised over $50 million. This money has funded more than 160 private grants for scientists whose only goal is victory over cancer. I know that Jimmy Valvano is smiling somewhere in the heavens because of what he left here on earth. But he is grinning most by that fact that Jamie Howard's prognosis calls for a "good, full and healthy life." Jamie Howard's maiden name, you may be interested in knowing, was Jamie Valvano...she is Jimmy Valvano's daughter.

The final piece to the gutsy journey is about being a part of something greater than ourselves, and in so doing, we never know about the life or lives we will save in this process.

Closing Comments...

Near the end of his life, the literary great George Bernard Shaw was asked what person in history he would most like to have been. His answer, "The George Bernard Shaw he might have been but never became."

Over the last several years there has been much debate in the men's Division I college basketball ranks concerning player graduation rates. The debate stems from the responsibility, or lack there of, of the head coach to ensure that players do in fact leave the institution after four years with a diploma. One coach who had been openly criticized for a very poor player graduation rate fired back during a recent press conference. He asked the pool of hungry reporters, "Who is able to graduate from our fine University?" After a short and dramatic pause, his eyes narrowed as a serious look emerged. Then he answered his own question, "Anyone who wants to."

"Whatever you can do or dream you can," Goethe once said, "begin it. Boldness has genius, power and magic in it."

As I was preparing all of the last minute details for this book, the cover design, the final editing, initial press mailings, etc., a friend reminded me of Aron Ralston and his incredible story. Do you remember Aron?

Aron was an avid outdoorsman and enjoyed mountain climbing. On a beautiful April day in 2003 he set out on a short excursion, out to the Utah Canyons. It was such a small outing that Aron went alone, and he didn't tell anyone where he was going.

During the climb, he went to move around an 800-pound boulder. As he did, for some unexplainable reason the boulder shifted, pinning his right hand beneath the large rock. There he was, stuck, trapped...alone.

Aron was not hanging on the side of a rock for mere hours; he was there for days, trapped for five days to be exact. In an interview sometime after the incident, Aron said, "After having enough sleep deprived, meandering thoughts about how I arrived in the canyon, I realized that [my situation] was the result of decisions that I had made. I chose to go out there by myself. I chose to not tell anyone where I was going. I chose not to go with [two climbers] I had met in the canyon [on the first day]." It was time for Aron to act...to climb out of the place that he had climbed into.

This action meant choosing life, and the only alternative in this case, was to cut off his hand at the wrist. Days of chipping on the rock to free the hand had not worked. He realized that it was his only choice for life. Later, when asked if it hurt (cutting off the hand), he said this, "Well, I didn't have any sensation in my right hand from the time of the accident onward. However, I did feel pain coming from the area where the boulder rested on my wrist. When I amputated, I felt every bit of it. It hurt to break the bone, and it certainly hurt to cut the nerve. But cutting the muscle was not as bad. Overall, it was a hundred times worse than any pain I've felt before. It recalibrated what I'd understood pain to be. At the same time, it was also the most beautiful thing I've ever felt."

Life is a mountain, one with no crest. It is about climbing, reaching a plateau and then moving on, up to new heights. Sometimes we get stuck on our climb, trapped by a boulder. In life, this boulder can be any number of things that limit our ascent: fear, greed, guilt, resentment, material 'stuff,' insecurity, drink, food, perceived lack of time, television, harmful relationships just to name a few. The only real question on this climb in life is: How long will our five days be? How long will we choose to remain trapped, hanging on the side of life's mountain?

As we reach the end of this book together, we have a choice. We can continue to hang, trapped by the things in this world; or we can do what Aron did, we can cut ourselves free. While we may not experience the same physical pain as Aron, in an emotional sense the pain will make us "recalibrate" what we call pain. Amputating those areas that hold us back is the same as cutting off a limb. They are a part of us; we think we need them to live and can't go on without them...it is real pain. In the midst of our pain and doubt however beauty will emerge...just ask Aron.

Today is graduation day if we want it to be. Today we can cut free and move up our mountain. The truth about this book, the stories and the concepts they teach, is that none of them are new. That's the reality about any motivational or self-help type material. In our hearts we know all of these things and more, much more. If we need more time, it's okay to take it. If we need another day, another year, another book before we cut free and climb higher, that is acceptable. But know, too, that we don't need another book or more time...we have what we need for success, to be gutsy. We can today graduate. Using the concepts in this book to rekindle the truth in our heart, today we can cut free that which holds us back.

In the end, this climb up life's mountain isn't a race but a personal challenge to be who we really are, to reach new heights, our potential. Near the end of his life, the literary master George Bernard Shaw was asked what person in history he would most like to have been. His answer, "The George Bernard Shaw he might have been but never became." How long will our five days be? Who will graduate? Anyone who wants to!

Bibliography

Collins, Jim, *Good to Great, Why Some Companies Make the Lead...and Others Don't.* New York: Harper Collins Publishing, 2001.

Moore, Thomas, *Dark Nights of the Soul: A Guide to Finding Your Way Through Life's Ordeals.* New York: Gotham Books, 2004.

Walsch, Neale Donald, *Moments of Grace.* Virginia: Hampton Roads Publishing Company, Inc., 2001.

Trump, Donald, *Think Like a Billionaire: Everything You Need to Know About Success, Real Estate, and Life.* New York: Random House, Inc., 2004.

Krzyzewski, Mike, *Leading with the Heart: Coach K's Successful Strategies for Basketball, Business, and Life.* New York: Warner Brothers, Inc., 2000.

Ralston, Aron, *Between a Rock and a Hard Place.* New York, Atria Books, 2004.

GUTSY (<u>G</u>o <u>U</u>ntil <u>T</u>ime <u>S</u>tops <u>Y</u>ou!) 142

Meeting Matt; about the author...

You have either just finished this book or you have done what I do when picking up a book for the first time, immediately turn to the back. Either way, thanks for picking up the book. If you did just finish the book, you really don't need to 'meet' me as we have already been introduced through many stories in the book.

What is most exciting, however, isn't discussed in these pages. It is the creation of K-Crof Industries, LLC in 2006; an organization dedicated to building people through writing, speaking and giving. I serve as K-Crof's Director. We are working hard to 'build people' through the use of life, light, and laughter in each inspirational presentation and through products like this book. To learn more about me, to order additional copies of this or my other books, or to give me feedback concerning this book, please log onto our website, www.thesafetysoul.org

Thanks again for reading this book! God bless and Godspeed as you work toward living the life that matches your true value...Matt.

K-Crof Products; Order Sheet:

- ❑ ***ISMA (Involved Safety Meeting Activities) –101 Ways to Get Your People Involved!*** -It doesn't matter if you manage a safety sensitive job or a sales team, this book can change your training and meeting culture...
- ❑ ***The Safety Soul, Quotes and Stories to Inspire Safety and Life*** – What comes from the heart goes to the heart; and in safety we don't manage assets like tools or equipment, we manage relationships...this book can help make the difference.
- ❑ ***GUSTY*** -The official 'I can' handbook. This book gets you and your organization 'in' to success.

Books may be purchased via the internet: www.thesafetysoul.org or by calling K-Crof's offices, (573) 999-7981. Discounts for volume orders.

Presentations and Keynote Address; Contact Matt to learn more about his speaking and consulting services. Contact Matt directly via his website, www.thesafetysoul.org, email; matt@thesafetysoul.org or phone; 573.999.7981.